The Rockwool Foundation Research Unit

The Price of Prejudice

Morten Hedegaard and Jean-Robert Tyran

University Press of Southern Denmark
Odense 2011

The Price of Prejudice

Study Paper No. 32

Published by:
© The Rockwool Foundation Research Unit and
University Press of Southern Denmark

Copying from this book is permitted only within
institutions that have agreements with CopyDan,
and only in accordance with the limitations laid
down in the agreement

Address:
The Rockwool Foundation Research Unit
Sølvgade 10
DK-1307 Copenhagen K

Telephone	+45 33 34 48 00
Fax	+45 33 34 48 99
E-mail	forskningsenheden@rff.dk
Home page	www.rff.dk
ISBN	978-87-90199-53-1
ISSN	0908-3979
May 2010	
Print run:	300
Printed by	Special-Trykkeriet Viborg a-s
Price:	60.00 DKK, including 25% VAT

Contents

Abstract 5
1. Introduction 6
2. Measuring ethnic discrimination in the work place 9
3. Experimental design 12
4. Results 19
4.1 The price of taste-based discrimination 19
4.2 Taste-based discrimination 23
4.3 Discrimination when both types of prejudice can matter 28
5. Concluding remarks 36
References 39
Appendices 42
Appendix A: Flyer used for recruiting 43
Appendix B: Location and participants 44
Appendix C: Description of the work task 47
Appendix D: Validation of classification of first names .. 48
Appendix E: Using productivity differences as proxy for the price of discrimination 49
Appendix F: Robustness of price effect with respect to the decision maker's productivity 50
Appendix G: Testing for random assignment of price (simulation) 52
Appendix H: Eliciting productivity beliefs 54
Appendix I: Decomposition of the earnings gap 55

The Price of Prejudice

Morten Hedegaard and Jean-Robert Tyran[*]

Ethnic prejudice can result in "taste-based" or "statistical" discrimination in the workplace. We disentangle the two types of discrimination in a field experiment. We find that taste-based discrimination is common but remarkably responsive to the price of prejudice, i.e. to the opportunity cost of choosing a less productive worker on ethnic grounds. In addition, we find that accurate statistical discrimination fails to explain observed choices, and that taking ethnic prejudice into account helps to predict the incidence of discrimination.

Keywords: field experiment, discrimination, labor market.

JEL-codes: C93, J71

---

[*] Hedegaard: University of Copenhagen, Department of Economics, Øster Farimagsgade 5, building 26, DK-1353 Copenhagen K. Morten.Hedegaard@econ.ku.dk.
Tyran: University of Vienna, Department of Economics, Hohenstaufengasse 9, A-1010 Vienna, and CEPR (London). Jean-Robert.Tyran@econ.ku.dk.
We gratefully acknowledge generous financial support by the Rockwool Foundation. We are particularly grateful to Research Director Torben Tranæs for sparking our interest in this topic by drawing our attention to weaknesses of traditional experimental approaches to discrimination in the labor market. We are grateful for Torben's ongoing encouragement and support for the novel experimental procedures we developed and implemented. We also thank Dirk Engelmann, Simon Gächter and Ernesto Reuben for helpful comments and student assistants Nete Daly, Pelle Flachs and Anne Schjellerup Olsen for their practical support in conducting the experiment.

Introduction

Public debate is rightly concerned with ethnic discrimination in the work place because of its adverse consequences for the discriminated and for society at large. Ethnic discrimination is unfair to the discriminated, discourages investment in human capital and can lead to unemployment and even social unrest. Yet, this paper is not concerned with the adverse consequences of discrimination but with the economic causes of discrimination. In particular, we study the "price of prejudice" that discriminators pay for discrimination. Knowing whether discriminators pay such a price deliberately or unintentionally, and how they react to changes in that price is of utmost importance in designing effective policies to clamp down on discrimination.

Most of the economic literature has focused on "statistical discrimination" (Phelps 1972, Arrow 1973). This type of discrimination occurs if employers have imperfect information about the individual productivity of job candidates but can observe a group characteristic like ethnicity. If average productivity is indeed different across ethnic groups, an employer maximizes average profits by choosing the worker of the more productive ethnic group even if the individual job candidates are otherwise identical on observables. The literature usually assumes that employers form accurate judgments about the relative average productivity of workers by ethnic groups. Whether or not one likes to call such "accurate statistical discrimination" (ASD) prejudiced[1], it is clear that employers on average do not pay a price of prejudice when engaging in ASD.

In this paper, we investigate "prejudice" with two distinct meanings. First, ethnic prejudice can be belief-driven and result in inaccurate statistical discrimination. The employer may unintentionally pay a price of prejudice if he has false beliefs about average group

---

[1] Economist would typically not call accurate statistical discrimination prejudiced while laypeople (and legislators) often do. In the theory of statistical discrimination majority employers are not assumed to have any ethnic animus against minorities nor are they assumed to have biased beliefs about the average performance of minorities on the job. In that sense, it seems appropriate to say that employers are not prejudiced. However, employers do choose between individuals based on the (true, relative) productivity of ethnic groups. If the distributions of productivities for minority and majority workers are different but overlap, it happens with some probability that the employer does not hire the most productive candidate. In that sense, the employer can be said to be prejudiced against (highly productive) minority individuals. Note that statistical discrimination in the work place is illegal in most countries.

productivities or about the ability to collaborate on the job when workers have different ethnicity. Second, ethnic prejudice can be animus-driven resulting in "taste-based" discrimination (Becker 1957). For example, an employer may correctly believe that minority workers are on average more productive than majority workers but may dislike minority people for reasons that are unrelated to their productivity. Such an employer deliberately pays a price for his ethnic prejudice when hiring a majority worker at given wages.

The vast literature on ethnic discrimination in the work place (see Altonji and Blank 1999 for a survey) has struggled for decades with measuring the relevance of these two types of ethnic prejudice, essentially because beliefs and preferences cannot be directly observed. Experimental economists have developed tools to elicit beliefs and infer preferences from observed behavior in the laboratory but such measurement is fraught with difficulties if subjects are aware of being observed because of the illicit nature of discrimination. Researchers have developed clever designs (so-called correspondence tests and audit studies) to circumvent that problem using natural field experiments in which potential discriminators are not aware of being observed (e.g. Bertrand and Mullainathan 2004). However, such designs are not well suited to control the price of prejudice and, thus, to study how this price shapes discrimination choices.

We use a natural field experiment with two treatments to investigate the two types of prejudice and how they translate into hiring choices at given wages. In treatment Info, we identify taste-based discrimination by controlling for beliefs and by randomly assigning a price of discrimination. In essence, only animus-driven prejudice can matter for discrimination in Info because decision makers know the ethnicity and individual productivities of the job candidates. We randomly vary the price of discrimination by giving decision makers the choice between candidates of different productivities which allows us to estimate how taste-based discrimination responds to changes in its price. In treatment NoInfo, both taste-based and belief-based prejudice can matter for discrimination because decision makers do not know candidates' individual productivities and thus have to form beliefs about the average productivity of ethnic groups. In NoInfo, we investigate the relative predictive power of animus- and belief-driven prejudice by explaining the gap between observed behavior and the benchmark of "accurate statistical discrimination". To account for this gap, we elicit beliefs and use our estimate of taste-based discrimination from treatment Info. In both treatments, we take great care to run a natural field experiment, i.e. an experiment in which participants are not aware that they are in an experiment, to avoid possible bias in the measurement of morally sensitive (and illegal) ethnic discrimination.

The experiment proceeds as follows. We hire 169 juveniles from secondary schools in Copenhagen, Denmark, with Danish-sounding and Muslim-sounding names to pack letters for a large mailing and pay them at a piece rate. Workers are requested to show up for work twice in two consecutive weeks. In the first round, they work in isolation and we measure their individual productivity on the job. Before they come back for the second round, we call randomly selected workers on the phone and inform them that they will again do the same job but now have to work in teams of two. They are informed that they are paid according to the same piece rate as in round one and share earnings from team output in round two with the other team member. These randomly selected workers can choose whom to work with. The choice is between a candidate from the ethnic majority group and a candidate from an ethnic minority group. In treatment Info, we provide the decision maker with information about the individual productivity of the two candidates, i.e. the number of letters packed in round one, and their first names as a marker of ethnicity. The candidates are randomly selected from the pool of workers and therefore have random productivity differences. Treatment NoInfo is the same as Info except that decision makers are not informed about candidates' individual productivities. We elicit beliefs about individual and team productivity on a different but similar sample. We use these beliefs to test if beliefs are accurate and to evaluate how much of the price of prejudice can be attributed to biased beliefs and animus, respectively.

In treatment Info, we find that taste-based discrimination is common even at a substantial cost and that the tendency to discriminate is not different across ethnic types. We find that discriminators are on average willing to forego 8 percent of their earnings in round two to work with a person of their own ethnic type. Our main result from treatment Info is that taste-based discrimination is surprisingly responsive to the price of prejudice. Our best estimate is an elasticity of -.9, i.e. we find that the probability to discriminate falls by about 9 percent if the price of discrimination goes up by 10 percent. These results suggest that policies aiming to clamp down on animus-driven discrimination by increasing the price of discrimination to employers may be rather effective.

In treatment NoInfo, we find that accurate statistical discrimination (ASD) fails to explain observed outcomes since we observe a large gap between observed earnings and earnings with ASD (about 4 percent of total output). To account for animus-driven prejudice, we use our

Both in-person audits and correspondence tests have important advantages, but concentrate on measuring the extent of discrimination when discrimination is free for the discriminator. Instead, we observe discrimination when there is a price to pay for being prejudiced, i.e. when discrimination is costly to the discriminator.[6] Our approach allows us to put a price tag on discrimination choices or, borrowing Gary Becker's (1957) expression[7], to estimate how discrimination responds to the "price of prejudice", rather than just observing that discrimination occurs when it is costless.

3   Experimental design

A general description of the experiment is as follows. We recruit an approximately balanced sample of juveniles with Danish-sounding and Muslim-sounding names from secondary schools in central Copenhagen for a letter packing job. Volunteers commit to show up twice for packing letters and indicate their availability for work. In the first round, they pack letters at a piece rate in isolation. This round serves to measure individual productivity on the job. In the second round, workers are required to work in teams of two, and some randomly selected workers (the "decision makers") can choose their partner. We construct triples of workers by randomly drawing one decision maker and two "candidates", one with a Danish-sounding name and one with a Muslim-sounding name.

The discrimination choice is made between rounds one and two. We call the decision makers on the phone and explain that they will do the same job at the same piece rate in round two, but have to work in teams of two. In treatment Info, they learn the first names and the productivity (i.e. number of letters packed in round one) of the two candidates. In treatment NoInfo, they only learn the first names. In both conditions, decision makers know that all

---

[6] Few studies have been able to relate variations in price to discrimination choices in a context not related to work. For example, Baccara et al. (2009) use variation in the cost of adopting children in the US to estimate the willingness to pay for babies with particular (ethnic, among others) characteristics. Pope and Sydnor (2011) use variation in interest rates in online peer-to-peer lending to show that statistical discrimination of black borrowers absent animus cannot explain net returns observed in loan-performance data. Levitt (2004) uses data from a TV show to test how statistical discrimination of candidates reacts to changes in cost.

[7] "Price and Prejudice" is the title of part 2 in Becker (1976, The economic approach to human behavior) which is a revised version of his PhD thesis, published in 1957.

Bertrand and Mullainathan (BM, 2004) is an excellent example of a correspondence test.[4] BM submit pairs of resumes to job openings in Chicago and Boston. The pairs of resumes are carefully matched such that they are as similar as possible with respect to productivity signals while keeping them distinct in a formal sense to avoid that employers realize that the resumes are fictitious. BM use a typical "White-sounding" and a "Black-sounding" name in each pair as a marker of ethnicity. BM find that applicants with White-sounding names are about 50 percent more likely to receive call-backs than applicants with Black-sounding names. In addition, of the 157 employers who responded asymmetrically to White-sounding and Black-sounding applications, 83 favored White-sounding applications while only 39 favored Black-sounding ones.

A particularly innovative aspect of BM is their ability to benchmark the returns of having a White-sounding name. BM submit four resumes to each job opening, two similar ones of low quality and two of high quality. Quality differs along ten dimensions, for example with respect to years of experience or computer skills. This variation in quality allows BM to estimate "the return to a White name" which is found to be "equivalent to about eight additional years of experience" (p. 998). While such equivalents can be interpreted in terms of cost of discrimination to the discriminated they are difficult to interpret in terms of the price of prejudice paid by the discriminator which is the focus of our study.[5] The reason is that the opportunity cost of hiring a White worker of lower quality rather than a Black worker of high quality is not known to the researchers. While BM's main finding of a racial gap in callbacks is consistent with both animus-driven and belief-driven prejudice, the authors argue that neither theory can satisfactorily explain the full set of findings.

---

[4] Correspondence tests are available for about a dozen countries, and they yield, by and large, evidence of pronounced discrimination. For example, Carlsson and Rooth (2007) find callback rates are 50 percent higher for applicants with Swedish-sounding names compared to Middle Eastern-sounding names in Sweden, Oreopoulos (2009) finds that callback rates are 40 percent higher for applicants with English-sounding names than with Chinese-, Indian- or Pakistani-sounding names in Canada.

[5] Caruso et al. (2009) use a related technique, so-called conjoint analysis, to estimate how decision makers trade-off relevant (like education and IQ) and irrelevant (body weight) characteristics in choosing a team-mates for a hypothetical trivia contest. While the paper estimates a trade-off, it is silent on the price of prejudice paid by the discriminator because the choices were not consequential.

(i.e. actors) of different ethnicity are matched into pairs with respect to physical appearance and are trained to behave similarly in job interviews. For example, Pager, Western and Bonikowski (2009) study hiring in the low-wage labor market in New York and find that black applicants are about half as likely to receive callbacks or job offers as white applicants. Second, in correspondence tests, pairs of fictitious resumes are submitted to employers by mail. Discrimination is inferred from differential callback or job-offer rates across pairs of workers which are similar in all respects except for ethnicity. These approaches have the advantage of using controlled variation to isolate the causal effect of ethnicity on employers' responses (see List 2006 for a discussion). Controlling for productivity differences by making pairs of ethnically diverse candidates as similar as possible is appealing since observing unequal treatment of otherwise identical workers is closely tied to a common definition of discrimination.[3]

Despite their clear advantages, correspondence tests and in-person audits also have some limitations (see Pager 2007 for a discussion). A concern with in-person audits is that testers are usually informed about the purpose of the study which may induce them, perhaps unconsciously, to behave in ways that can distort findings. Another concern with in-person audits is that testers may differ in characteristics that seem relevant for their labor productivity to the employer but are not observed by the researcher (e.g. Heckman 1998). Essentially, the problem is that ethnicity cannot be randomly assigned to testers. This problem is circumvented by correspondence tests which make (fictitious) applications similar in the eyes of employers. But this strength is also a weakness of this approach. Since applicants are equally productive by design, discriminators do not pay a price for their prejudice and correspondence tests may therefore exaggerate the true extent of discrimination (e.g. Heckman and Siegelman 1993). In addition, correspondence tests are silent on how discrimination responds to changes in the price of discrimination because they usually do not vary the cost of choosing one candidate over the other (see Neumark 2010 for a discussion).

---

[3] Altonji and Blank (1999: 3168) define discrimination in the labor market as "a situation in which persons who provide labor market services and who are equally productive in a physical or material sense are treated unequally in a way that is related to an observable characteristic such as race, ethnicity, or gender".

estimate from treatment Info. To account for belief-driven prejudice, we use elicited beliefs. At least 40 percent of that gap is explained by animus-driven prejudice alone, and at most one third is explained by belief-driven prejudice alone. Jointly, the two types of prejudice explain about 60 percent of the gap. Thus, our results suggest that belief-driven and animus-driven ethnic prejudice are important causes of ethnic discrimination in the workplace, and need to be taken into account above and beyond the theory of accurate statistical discrimination.

The paper is organized as follows. Section 2 discusses related literature, section 3 describes our experimental design, and section 4 presents the results. Section 5 summarizes and concludes.

2   Measuring ethnic discrimination in the work place

The traditional econometric approach to measuring the effects of discrimination is to estimate a "wage gap" between a minority and a majority group based on observables such as education or years of experience on the job (see Altonji and Blank 1999 for a survey). However, attributing the entire unexplained part of such regressions to discrimination is problematic, mainly because the true economic value of a worker (the marginal product of labor) is not observed by the researcher. Such approaches only allow for indirect inference of whether discrimination is taste-based or driven by false beliefs, and such inference is fraught with difficulties. For example, List (2006: 19) notes that "An important lesson learned from the vast literature on discrimination is that data availability places severe constraints on efforts to understand the nature of discrimination, forcing researchers to speculate about the source of the observed discrimination."

Field experiments[2] circumvent this difficulty and have been used for more than 40 years to investigate the causes of ethnic discrimination in the work place (Daniel 1968 and Jowell and Prescott-Clarke 1970 are early examples. See Riach and Rich 2002 for a survey). Such field experiments traditionally come in one of two guises. First, in in-person audit studies, "testers"

---

[2] There is also a considerable literature on discrimination using laboratory research both in psychology and economics (e.g. Gneezy and Fershtman 2001 or Holm 2001; see Anderson, Fryer and Holt 2006). Field experiments have also been used to measure gender discrimination (e.g. Goldin and Rouse 2000) and other types of discrimination in the labor market (e.g. Neumark et al. 1996), and discrimination in other markets (e.g. Ayres and Kenny 1995, Levitt 2004, List 2004, Yinger 1998).

candidates are equally experienced and have similar characteristics. In particular, they know that all candidates have worked on the same job under identical conditions and that they are recruited from secondary schools. When the decision maker has made a choice, we call the chosen candidate requesting him or her to show up at a particular time. In round two, teams are formed according to the choices of the decision makers whenever possible, and workers are paid out for both rounds.

We took great care to implement a proper natural field experiment – in which participants are not aware that they are part of an experiment. In particular, we have been careful at all stages of the experiment to assure that the job itself and the work conditions appear natural to participants, that the experiment (in particular the information provided to decision makers) is tightly controlled, and that all aspects of the experiment are consequential and do not involve deception.

Detailed description of procedures

Recruiting. We distributed hundreds of flyers in eleven upper secondary schools in central Copenhagen.[8] The flyer explains that the University of Copenhagen is looking for part-time workers to prepare a major mailing for research purposes. The flyer also explains that applicants are expected to show up for two hours in each of two consecutive weeks. Applicants are requested to call us on a phone number indicated on the flyer.

We recruited in upper secondary schools because these juveniles have relatively low outside options, are similar with respect to age (16-20 years old) and education, are legally allowed to work for money, and because there is considerable naturally occurring ethnic heterogeneity in this group (23% of juveniles in these schools are immigrants). Using a homogenous subject pool has the advantage of minimizing unobserved heterogeneity across ethnic types, for example with respect to language skills. In addition, it is feasible to recruit an approximately balanced sample by gender from this pool. The reason for wanting a balanced sample is that we keep the triples (see below) separate by gender to avoid confound of ethnicity and gender.

Names as markers of ethnicity. Upon calling us, we record the applicants' names, phone numbers, and where they saw the flyer. Applicants indicate when they are available for work in

---

[8] The flyer is reprinted in appendix A. Appendix B shows the location of the schools.

both rounds and are requested to make a commitment to show up at any of these slots. We classify the applicants according to their first names as Danish-sounding or Muslim-sounding. We call 169 persons with high availability[9], with names apt to evoke ethnic stereotypes, and in approximately balanced proportions (see table 1).[10]

We called applicants with typical Danish-sounding and Muslim-sounding names because these ethnic groups are by far the largest in Denmark.[11] We use first names as markers of ethnicity since it is natural to refer to a person in Denmark by first name across all social strata. Using first names to evoke stereotypes is common practice in correspondence tests. These tests use fictitious first names which can be chosen to be particularly strong markers of ethnicity (e.g. Lakisha vs. Emily in Bertrand and Mullainathan 2004). In contrast, we use participants' actual first names to mark ethnicity. In a follow-up study with 144 subjects, we find that our ethnic markers are highly effective and confound rarely occurs. For example, names we classify as Muslim-sounding are thought to be Danish-sounding only in about 1 percent of the cases (see appendix D for details).

Note that the first names of the ethnic minority group are both Muslim-sounding but also foreign-sounding to Danish ears. Thus, our study cannot not provide a definitive answer on whether the animus we measure among Danes is directed at Muslims or foreigners living in Denmark more generally. However, a correspondence tests designed to investigate this issue (Adida et al. 2010) for France suggests that animus against Muslims is more pronounced than animus against foreigners in general.[12]

---

[9] 95 percent ($n = 169$) of participants were available 3 or more days, 55 percent on 6 or more days in round 2.

[10] Table 1 shows that the names of 7 workers did not fit either ethnic type. These workers (and the teams they worked in) are excluded from our analysis below. Table 1 does not list 27 workers who participated in a pre-test. These workers were recruited from a school where we did not recruit for the main experiment.

[11] According to official statistics (2009, www.statistikbanken.dk), 69 percent of immigrants in Denmark are from non-Western countries, and most of these originate from countries with high proportions of Muslims such as Turkey, Iraq and Pakistan.

[12] The study combines a foreign-sounding last name (Diouf, a typical name in Senegal) either with a Christian (Marie) or Muslim (Khadija) first name. Response rates for Marie Diouf and a reference candidate with a typical French name (Aurélie Ménard) were not different. However, response rates for Khadija Diouf were significantly lower than for Marie Diouf.

Table 1: Number of workers in round 1 by gender and ethnicity

	Ethnicity			
Gender	Danish-sounding name	Muslim-sounding name	Other name	Total
Female	40	46	5	*91*
Male	40	36	2	*78*
Total	*80*	*82*	*7*	*169*

Measuring individual productivity. A total of 169 persons work in round 1 of our experiment. Workers are requested to show up at particular times and are led to separate rooms to minimize interaction between them. The letter packing job is explained and demonstrated to each worker individually. The job involves packing letters marked with an ID-number. These numbers have to be looked up in a binder and are associated with different letter types. Depending on the type, letters have to be complemented with a gift and sorted into specific bins (see appendix C for details). When participants indicate that they understand the task, the payment scheme (the piece rate is DKK 4, approx. 0.5€ per letter), and that they are ready to start, an alarm clock is set in the control room (see Figure B2 in appendix B). After exactly 90 minutes a staff person returns to the worker and counts the number of letters packed. Each worker got a receipt confirming their entitlement and was paid at the end of round 2 to provide them with incentives to return.

The letter packing job is ideal for our purposes for several reasons. First, the job is easy to explain and easy to learn for juveniles within the given time frame. Second, the job can meaningfully be done both in isolation and in a team of two workers. Third, teamwork on the job requires minimal spoken interaction which minimizes the motive to discriminate against members from a different "speech community" (e.g. Lang 1986). Fourth, the task produces sufficient variation in individual output which is essential to make discrimination costly. Fifth, the job is not artificial. It is not unusual for juveniles to work in a temporary job like letter packing and the job is real in the sense that we effectively used the letters packed for a large-scale mailing.[13]

Matching procedure. Upon completion of round 1, we match workers into triples as follows. We randomly select a person to be the decision maker. Thus, the decision maker may have a Danish-sounding or a Muslim-sounding name. We then determine the set of all suitable candidates for this decision maker. This is the set of participants who are of the same gender as the decision maker, are from a different school, and are available for work on at least one of the time slots indicated by the decision maker. We randomly draw two candidates from this set. One candidate is of the same ethnic type as the decision maker (*same* for short), one is of the other type (*other* for short). In treatment Info, the draws are repeated until *same* is *less* productive than *other* and the two candidates are available on different weekdays. If no such pair exists, we randomly draw a new decision maker from the pool.

We randomly draw decision makers to observe discrimination choices by both ethnic types. The ability to observe discrimination choices by minority decision makers is, to the best of our knowledge, a unique feature of this study. For example, correspondence tests usually do not observe the ethnicity of the employer and simply assume that he or she belongs to the ethnic majority. We match candidates and decision makers from different schools to exclude that they personally know each other, thus avoiding confound of ethnic discrimination with a preference for a personal acquaintance. We are able to match teams from different schools because we gather information about school affiliation from participants when they apply for the job over the phone. Randomly drawing two candidates serves to generate a random price of discrimination (i.e. the earnings foregone by choosing *same* over *other*). Randomly matching the candidates with a decision makers serves to make price independent of any animus that may be present. Random assignment of price to decision makers is a precondition for identifying taste-based discrimination, as is discussed in more detail in section 4.1 and appendix G. The restriction imposed in Info that *same* has lower productivity than *other* serves to maximize the number of informative choices. Choices are informative in the sense that decision makers with strong animus are likely to be detected. The reason why the candidates must be available on

---

[13] We used the letters packed for a mailing to recruit participants for a large-scale internet study. This study used different letter types necessitating sorting the letters. We randomly checked 5 letters for each participant in round 1. The error rate was low (0.05) and did not differ by ethnic type ($p = 0.270$, χ^2-test). Error rates also do not differ by team composition in round 2 ($p = 0.688$, χ^2-test).

different weekdays is that we frame the discrimination choice as a choice between two weekdays rather than between two persons, as is explained next.

Discrimination choice. The discrimination choice is made on the phone prior to round 2. Upon answering the phone, the decision maker is asked to confirm availability on the two time slots determined by the matching procedure (Tuesday and Wednesday 2 p.m. - 4 p.m., say). If the decision maker cannot reconfirm availability, we say we have to make new arrangements and call back later. In this case, the triple pertaining to this decision maker is reinserted into the pool and a new triple is drawn according to the matching procedure described above. If the answer is affirmative, decision makers are informed that the job in round 2 is the same and is paid according to the same piece rate as in round 1. They are told that, unlike in round 1, they have to work in teams of two and that they have to share the revenue from teamwork.[14] Decision makers are told that which person they are going to work with depends on which day they choose. In treatment Info, the decision makers are told the first names and the number of letters packed in round 1 for both candidates and asked to make a choice. For example, "If you choose Tuesday, you will work with Ahmed who packed 150 letters last week. If you choose Wednesday, you will work with Christian who packed 110 letters last week. So, when would you like to work, Tuesday or Wednesday at 2 p.m.?" In treatment NoInfo, the procedure is the same except that we do not mention the individual output of candidates in round 1.[15]

An important advantage of this procedure is the high degree of control it provides over the information available to the decision makers. In both treatments, decision makers know that candidates are similar (they are recruited from the same set of schools) and have the same experience on the job (they all worked in round 1 under the exact same conditions). Beyond that, in treatment Info, the decision makers know *only* the names and productivities of the candidates. Since they cannot personally identify or see the candidates, factors such as attractiveness or personal appearance cannot affect decisions in our design (see e.g. Möbius and Rosenblat 2006 for experimental and Hamermesh and Biddle 1994 for field evidence on personal attractiveness and discrimination). We frame the discrimination choice as a choice of

---

[14] If asked, we justified that the job has to be done in teams of two by explaining that "we found out that working in teams of two is more effective and therefore workers on average earn more than last week". We knew from a pretest with 27 participants that this claim is true.

[15] Non-chosen candidates were reinserted into the pool of participants and were matched into another triple, either as decision maker or candidate. Thus, our design does not necessarily imply a cost to the discriminated.

workdays rather than persons to minimize so-called Hawthorne or experimenter demand effects (see Zizzo 2010 for a general discussion). Such effects may result from participants' concerns to conform with notions of political correctness (see e.g. Kawakami et al. 2009).

Credibility and consequentiality. We take great care to create a natural setting, to measure output and to provide information with tight control, to insure that all information provided to decision makers is truthful, and that choices are consequential. For example, decision makers were presented with a choice between two real people, we indicate their actual first names, and their actual productivity in round 1. Decision makers are matched to work with the partner of their choice in round 2 whenever possible (i.e. when both show up on time) which implies that the chosen candidate cannot make a discrimination choice.

We believe that our choice of the location and work task was highly credible in the sense that workers did not know that they were participating in an experiment. We made choices consequential for two reasons. First, consequentiality serves to avoid deception and disappointment. For example, decision makers who opt for a highly productive co-worker would be antagonized if forced to work with a low-productive partner in round 2. Second, the ability to observe team output in round 2 allows us to identify taste-based discrimination in treatment Info by controlling for a particular type of (team-work related) ethnic prejudice, as is explained next.

Team output in round 2 can in principle depend on the individual productivity of team members and the ethnic mix of the team. Because we observe output in round 2, we can test if that is the case. We show in section 4.1 that team output is very much driven by individual productivity in round 1, but does not depend on the ethnic team composition. That is, we find that the team production function is not "type specific". But decision makers may falsely believe that it is. For example, despite being told in Info that *same* is less productive when working in isolation than *other*, a decision maker may believe that team output is higher when working with *same* rather than *other* because "different types don't work together well". If so, observing a choice of *same* over *other* in Info is not an indication of taste-based discrimination but of a false belief. Therefore, we need to control for beliefs about the type-specificity of the team production function to correctly identify taste-based discrimination. Section 4.3 shows that the team production function is not believed to be type-specific. Since the team production function is in fact not type specific and is not believed to be, beliefs are correct in this dimension, and choosing *same* over *other* in Info is therefore a clear indication of taste-based discrimination.

4 Results

Section 4.1 estimates the price of taste-based discrimination, i.e. the earnings foregone by choosing *same* over *other* in Info, using a team production function. We find that the team production function is not type-specific which implies that discriminators pay a positive price for discrimination (i.e. choosing *same*) in Info. We argue that this price is known to decision makers since round 1 productivity is an excellent predictor of the price.

Section 4.2 presents the results for treatment Info. We find that 38 percent of decision makers engage in taste-based discrimination and they pay a price of about €5 on average. Importantly, we find that the probability to discriminate falls with its price and that the tendency to discriminate is not different across ethnic types after controlling for its price. We also estimate a distribution of the willingness to pay for taste-based discrimination.

Section 4.3 presents results for treatment NoInfo, i.e. when both animus-driven and belief-driven prejudice can matter for discrimination. We report results from a complementary study eliciting beliefs on production. We find that the team production function is not thought to be type specific, i.e. we find no evidence for prejudice about the ability to collaborate across types. However, we find that beliefs are biased in the sense that true productivity differences across ethnic types are underestimated. We find that accurate statistical discrimination (ASD) fails to account for observed choices. In fact, observed earnings are lower than those implied by ASD and about 60 percent of that gap is accounted for by animus and biased beliefs jointly. Thus, our estimate of taste-based discrimination from Info together with elicited beliefs predicts observed choices much more accurately than ASD.

4.1 The price of taste-based discrimination

We define the price of taste-based discrimination to the discriminator in Info as earnings foregone by choosing a less productive co-worker of the same ethnic type rather than a more productive worker of the other ethnic type. To measure this price, we estimate a team production function showing how workers with particular productivities in round 1 map into output of ethnically homogeneous and heterogeneous teams in round 2. We then estimate for each decision maker the marginal product of labor for the two candidates. This analysis yields the important result that team production is not type-specific, i.e. that two workers with given individual productivities produce the same output independent of the ethnic composition of the team. This result implies that a decision maker has a clear monetary incentive to choose the more productive candidate which, in treatment Info, is by design *other*. In other words, there is a price to pay for choosing *same*. If this price is known to the decision maker, a choice of *same* is a clear indication of taste-based discrimination, assuming utility maximizing choices. We argue that decision makers had almost perfect knowledge about the price in Info because candidates' round 1 productivities are excellent predictors of this price.

Figure 1: Production in round 1 and round 2

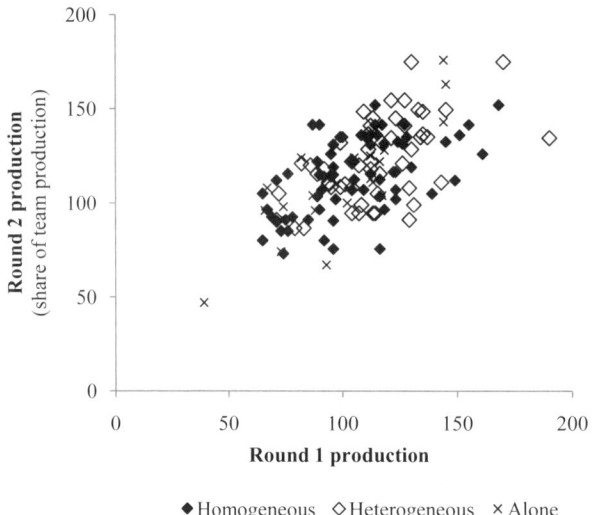

Note: The figure shows the number of letters packed in isolation in round 1 and the share of letters packed in round 2 for individuals who worked in round 2 in homogeneous teams (black diamonds, $n = 68$), in heterogeneous teams (white diamonds, $n = 52$), or alone (crosses, $n = 20$). The share is 50% of team output for those working in teams, and 100% of individual output for those working alone.

Figure 1 shows a scatterplot of worker i's share of production in round 2 (i.e. half of the letters jointly packed) by production in round 1 (i.e. letters packed in isolation). Black diamonds represent individuals in heterogeneous teams (52 individuals) and white diamonds represent individuals in homogenous teams (36 both Danish-sounding, 32 both Muslim-sounding). Crosses represent individuals working alone in round 2 (20 individuals) because they or their partner did not show up on time. The figure shows that there is considerable variation in both round 1 production (the average is 107 letters packed, sdv = 24) and in round 2 (average 115, sdv = 24). As expected by virtue of random treatment allocation, decision makers' distributions of round 1 production are not different across treatments ($p = 0.528$, Kolmogorov-Smirnov test). Workers with Danish-sounding names tended to be more productive in round 1 than those with Muslim-sounding names (116 vs. 100, $p = 0.000$, Mann-Whitney test). This finding has important implications for our analysis in both treatments and is discussed in detail below.

We estimate the team production function using all observations of workers who completed both rounds[16] as

$$\ln(Y^i_{i,j}) = \beta_0 + \beta_1 \cdot \ln x_i + \beta_2 \cdot \ln x_{j, j \neq i} + \beta_3 \cdot \ln x_i \cdot Alone + \gamma \cdot \mathbf{X} + \varepsilon_i,$$

where $Y^i_{i,j}$ is worker i's share of the team output in round 2 when working with co-worker j. We estimate team production as a function of worker i's own production in round 1, x_i, the production of the co-worker j in round 1 (x_j), an interaction term to capture different learning effects when working alone ($Alone = 1$ and $x_j = 0$ if i is working alone in phase 2), and a vector of variables characterizing the team composition (e.g. by ethnic type).

Table 2 shows various estimates for the team production function. The positive coefficients in the first two lines show that teams tend to be more productive if their members have high productivity in round 1. The coefficients in the third line reflect learning by those working alone in round 2. These coefficients are very similar in size to the previous ones suggesting that there is no gain from specialization in our task since those who happened to work alone are on average equally productive as those working in teams.[17] The significant coefficient for *Male* shows that males are about 6 percent more productive than females in round 2. Taken together, round 1 output explains a considerable share of variation in team output (adjusted R^2 is about .61 in all specifications) which implies that the information available to decision makers is an excellent predictor for the price of discrimination.

---

[16] In total, 140 workers completed both rounds according to the description in section 3. Observations from teams with workers having names which do not fit either ethnic type are excluded from our regression.

[17] Average earnings are the same whether working alone or in a team in round 2, holding everything else constant ($p = 0.573$, t-test). The coefficients in the first three lines of specification A are very similar because the share of team output for worker i and j is the same (one half) by definition and the share for a worker i working alone is estimated assuming a team mate j with the same round 1 production as worker i.

Table 2: Team production function

Dependent variable: ln(prod$_{2i}$)	(A)	(B)	(C)	(D)
ln(prod$_{1i}$)	0.416***	0.408***	0.421***	0.419***
	(0.044)	(0.044)	(0.050)	(0.051)
ln(prod$_{1j}$)	0.416***	0.426***	0.421***	0.428***
	(0.044)	(0.045)	(0.050)	(0.050)
ln(prod$_{1i}$) · Alone	0.416***	0.424***	0.324***	0.327***
	(0.044)	(0.044)	(0.107)	(0.109)
Male	0.064***	0.063***	0.064***	0.064***
	(0.022)	(0.022)	(0.023)	(0.023)
Decision maker		-0.018		-0.017
		(0.024)		(0.030)
Alone			0.452	0.468
			(0.545)	(0.549)
Danish-sounding team			0.037	0.041
			(0.025)	(0.033)
Muslim-sounding team			-0.019	-0.010
			(0.035)	(0.039)
Decision maker · Heterogeneous				0.012
				(0.045)
Constant	0.841***	0.843***	0.785**	0.768**
	(0.219)	(0.220)	(0.315)	(0.317)
Adj. R^2	0.611	0.610	0.615	0.610
N	140	140	140	140

Notes: Dependent variable is (the logarithm of) the number of letters packed in round 2 by worker i if working alone ($n = 20$) or, if working in a team ($n = 120$), half of the number of letters packed by i's team. prod$_{1i}$ is the number of letters packed in round 1 by worker i, prod$_{1j}$ the number of letters packed by i's co-worker in round 2. *Alone* is a dummy set to 1 if worker i works alone in round 2, *Male* is worker i's gender, *Decision maker* indicates if worker i makes a choice of co-worker. The remaining dummies characterize team composition in round 2. Numbers in parentheses are robust standard errors. * $p < 0.10$, ** $p < 0.05$, *** $p < 0.01$

Model B adds the dummy variable *Decision maker*. The insignificant estimate suggests that selection is not a serious issue with respect to team production as decision makers (after controlling for individual productivities) do not have significantly different productivity from those who have no choice to make. This is true for decision makers in general as well as for decision makers selecting into heterogeneous teams (see interaction term *Decision maker· Heterogeneous* in model D). Models C and D add dummies for team composition to test if ethnically homogenous teams are more productive than heterogeneous teams (which is the reference category in the regression). The insignificant estimates show that the team production function is not type-specific. That is, given individual productivities, heterogeneous teams are equally productive as homogenous teams.

Taken together, the estimates on the production function show that much of the variation in team production is explained by one's own productivity and the productivity of the co-worker (which are both known when making the choice), but essentially nothing is explained by the ethnic type of the co-worker. This finding is important because it implies a monetary incentive to choose *other* in treatment Info. In other words, there is a price a to pay for discrimination, and decision makers had all the required information to know the price.

The price of taste-based discrimination is defined as earnings foregone by choosing to work with *same* rather than *other* in treatment Info. This price is not directly observed in our experiment because the decision maker only works with the chosen candidate but not with the non-chosen candidate. We thus have to estimate the counterfactual. In estimating the price of discrimination, we use specification A in table 2 because all variables included in the other models are insignificant. The price is then the difference between decision maker i's earnings with *other* minus the earnings with *same*[18]

$$Price_i = p(\hat{Y}^i_{i,other} - \hat{Y}^i_{i,same}) > 0 \; \forall \; i \; .$$

We find that the distribution of $Price_i$ (mirrored on 0) is normal ($p = 0.818$, Shapiro-Wilk; $p = 0.721$, Shapiro-Francia; $p = 0.901$, Skewness/Kurtosis test for normality), as is expected by virtue of random sampling of candidates.

4.2 Taste-based discrimination

Section A) below shows that the probability to discriminate falls as its price increases. Section B) estimates the willingness to pay for taste-based discrimination.

Before proceeding to estimation, we provide some descriptive statistics. Decision makers in treatment Info all face a positive price of discrimination by design, on average €6.7 (sd = €4.7). We observe that 38 percent of decision makers in treatment Info choose to discriminate,

---

[18] The price of discrimination expressed in Euros is obtained by multiplying the difference in output with p which is the product of the piece rate (DKK 4 per letter) and the exchange rate (0.13 Euro per DKK).

i.e. choose *same*. This result is novel since we show that taste-based discrimination is common even when decision makers face a positive and known price of discrimination.

A first finding supporting our claim that higher (randomly assigned) prices causally reduce discrimination is that discriminators face lower prices on average than non-discriminators (€4.9 vs. €7.8). Both a Kolmogorov-Smirnov test ($p = 0.091$) and Wilcoxon rank-sum test ($p = 0.052$) show that prices are different for the two groups (see appendix G for tests showing that prices are randomly assigned). The average expected price of €4.9 for discriminators may seem low in absolute terms but is strikingly high in relative terms. For example, the average discriminator gives up 8 percent of round 2 earnings to work with *same* for 90 minutes.

A) The demand for taste-based discrimination

We estimate the demand for discrimination using a revealed preference approach. Assuming $Price_i$ is known to decision makers[19] and choices are utility maximizing, decision maker *i* reveals to have a "taste" for discrimination $a_i \geq Price_i$ if he chooses *same*. In this case, we say the decision maker engages in taste-based discrimination (and we assign a value $Discr = 1$). Conversely, the decision maker reveals to have $a_i < Price_i$ if he chooses *other*, and we say the decision maker does not discriminate ($Discr = 0$). Given a distribution of animus a in the sample, utility maximization implies that fewer decision makers prefer to discriminate as its price increases. In other words, the demand for discrimination is downward-sloping.

We regress the probability of observing discrimination ($Discr = 1$) on the price of discrimination as defined in section 4.1 (plus other controls explained below) as follows[20]

$$\Pr(Discr_i = 1 \mid \mathbf{X}) = \Phi(\mathbf{X}'\beta + \varepsilon_i).$$

Model (1) in table 3 provides the most parsimonious specification showing that the law of demand holds for taste-based discrimination. The coefficient on *Price* shows that discrimination falls by 3.6 percent if the price of discrimination goes up by €1. Note that this number is our best estimate for the average marginal change. Due to the non-linearity of the

---

[19] Below, we use the estimation results from the team production function to calculate *Price*. This implicitly assumes that decision makers know the team production function. Appendix D shows that our results are robust to this assumption. In particular, Appendix D shows that using raw productivity differences between candidates in round 1 as a proxy for *Price* yields the same qualitative results as those reported in table 3.

[20] We report probit estimates throughout the paper. Logit regressions yield qualitatively similar results.

demand relation, this marginal effect is not informative for larger changes in cost. We provide estimates for such changes in the discussion of figure 2.

Table 3: The demand for taste-based discrimination

Dependent variable: Discr	(1)	(2)	(3)	(4)
Price	-0.036**	-0.035**	-0.034**	-0.038*
	(0.016)	(0.017)	(0.016)	(0.020)
Danish-sounding		0.020		-0.045
		(0.160)		(0.286)
Male		-0.056		-0.022
		(0.152)		(0.284)
Danish-sounding · Price			0.005	0.011
			(0.022)	(0.040)
Male · Price			-0.007	-0.004
			(0.018)	(0.036)
R^2	0.082	0.085	0.086	0.087
N	37	37	37	37

Notes: The table shows average marginal effects estimated from Probit regressions. Numbers in parentheses are robust standard errors. *Discr* = 1 for a decision maker choosing *same* and 0 otherwise. *Male* and *Danish-sounding* are dummies characterizing the decision maker. * $p < 0.10$, ** $p < 0.05$, *** $p < 0.01$

Model (2) adds dummy variables for gender (*Male*) and ethnic type (*Danish-sounding*) of the decision maker. The insignificant estimate on *Danish-sounding* indicates that the tendency to discriminate is not different across ethnic types, after controlling for differences in prices. We think that this is a remarkable result for two reasons. First, attention both in the literature and policy debates usually focuses on discrimination of the minority group by the majority group because the adverse consequences of discrimination (for the discriminated and society at large) are more pronounced in this case. In fact, members of the majority group are more often in the position to discriminate, and workers from the minority group tend to be disadvantaged. However, our results suggest that observing more frequent discrimination of minorities may be simply due to the fact that majority decision makers have more opportunities to discriminate rather than a stronger ethnic animus.

Second, this result highlights the importance of controlling for prices when measuring discrimination. From simply looking at discrimination percentages, a layperson may be misled to conclude that decision makers with Danish-sounding names are more likely to discriminate. In fact, decision makers with Danish-sounding names discriminate in 44 percent of the cases, while those with Muslim-sounding names do so in only 33 percent of the cases (however, $p = 0.517$, χ^2 test). Yet, these differences do not reflect differences in animus because decision makers with Danish-sounding names face a lower price on average than decision makers with Muslim-sounding names (€5.2 vs. €7.8, $p = 0.078$, KS). The reason is that workers with Danish-sounding names are systematically more productive (116 letters) in round 1 than participants with Muslim-sounding names (100 letters). According to regressions (2) and (4) in table 3, these price differences explain the observed differences in taste-based discrimination across ethnic types (*Danish-sounding* is insignificant, but *Price* is significant).

Model (3) adds the interaction terms *Danish-sounding · Price*, and *Male · Price*. The respective estimates are insignificant, suggesting that responses to changes in price are not different across ethnic types and gender. Model (4) combines (2) and (3) and yields the same results.

Figure 2: The demand for discrimination

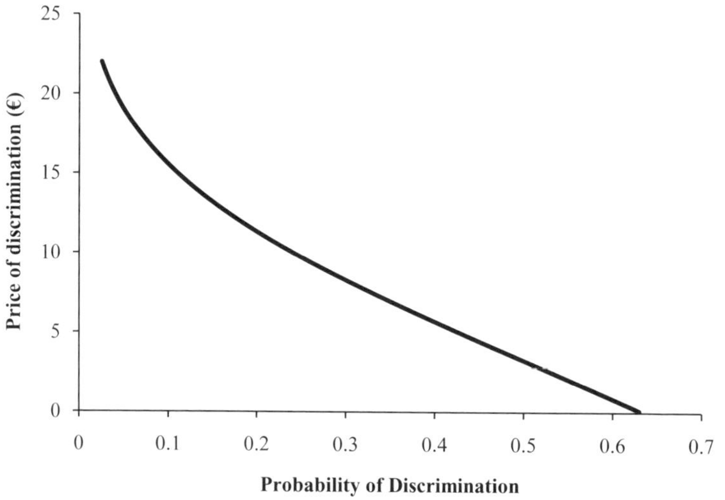

Notes: The figure shows the relation between the probability of discrimination (choosing *same*) in Info and the price of discrimination, calculated using specification (1) in table 3.

Figure 2 summarizes our main finding. Decision makers respond strongly to changes in prices. For example, the figure shows that increasing the price of discrimination by one standard deviation from the average (i.e. from €6.7 to €11.4) reduces the probability of discrimination by 45 percent (from .36 to .20). Conversely, decreasing the price by one standard deviation from the average (i.e. from €6.7 to €2.0) increases the probability by 54 percent (from

.36 to .55). Another way to describe the remarkable price-responsiveness is to estimate an elasticity which indicates the percentage decrease in the probability to discriminate in response to a 1% increase in price. Our best estimate is -0.9. This elasticity is an average of all elasticities, evaluated at each observation. In conclusion, we find that the demand for taste-based discrimination is downward-sloping and is surprisingly elastic.[21]

B) Willingness to pay for taste-based discrimination

An alternative representation our main finding is in terms of the willingness to pay for taste-based discrimination. According to the revealed preference approach described above, decision maker i reveals to have willingness to pay $a_i \geq Price_i$ if he chooses *same*. Conversely, the decision maker reveals to have $a_i < Price_i$ if he chooses *other*. We assume that willingness to pay is normally distributed in the population, $a_i \sim N(\mu_a, \sigma_a^2)$. We estimate μ_a and σ_a from estimated $Price_i$ (using model A in table 2) and observed discrimination choices as follows. We define the probability of discrimination as

$$\Pr(Discr = 1 | Price_i) = \Pr(a_i \geq Price_i)$$
$$= 1 - \Pr(a < Price_i)$$
$$= 1 - F_a(Price_i)$$

where F_a is the CDF of a. We use probit estimation to estimate this probability (see model 1 in table 3):

$$\Pr(Discr = 1 | Price_i) = \Phi(\beta_0 + \beta_1 \cdot Price_i + \varepsilon_i)$$

and use the estimates $(\hat{\beta}_0, \hat{\beta}_1)$ to obtain the distribution of the willingness to pay:

$$F_a(x) = 1 - \Phi(\hat{\beta}_0 + \hat{\beta}_1 \cdot x), x \in \Re$$

We find that the average decision maker in our sample is willing to pay μ_a = €3.2 to work with *same* rather than *other* (σ_a = €9.6). Our estimation approach allows decision makers to have positive (a dislike of *other*) or negative (a preference for *other*) animus. Interestingly, our estimate suggests that while a majority (63 percent) dislikes working with *other*, a considerable share also prefers working with *other*.

---

[21] Interestingly, our estimate at a price of zero is close to the estimates in correspondence tests. For example, we find that a decision maker with a majority name picks *same* with a probability of 63 percent at a zero price. Bertrand and Mullainathan (2004) find that workers with White names are about 50% more likely to be called back which, assuming that employers are White, translates into a 60 percent probability of choosing *same*.

4.3 Discrimination when both types of prejudice can matter

In treatment NoInfo, decision makers do not know candidates' individual productivity but do know their ethnic types. Thus, decision makers need to form beliefs about the relative productivity of workers across types to make optimal discrimination choices. Differences in beliefs about relative productivity are likely to be mainly driven by ethnicity in our design. The reason is that decision makers know that all candidates have very similar age and educational background (because they are recruited from the same set of schools) and have the exact same amount of experience with the work task. We thus control information and make the candidates similar – except for their ethnicity – in the eyes of the decision makers.

Accurate statistical discrimination (ASD) assumes that decision makers form rational (i.e. on average correct) beliefs and that decision makers have no animus.[22] That is, ASD assumes profit-maximizing choices. ASD predicts that all decision makers in NoInfo choose the candidate with a Danish-sounding name because these workers are on average more productive (116 vs. 100 letters packed in round 1). We find that ASD grossly mispredicts choices. In fact, about half of the choices are for the less profitable type, and decision makers with Muslim-sounding names are particularly prone to make such choices.

Treatment NoInfo serves to evaluate the predictive power of ASD against animus-driven and belief-driven prejudice in explaining observed outcomes. Such a comparative test is demanding because it requires that the researcher measures animus and rational beliefs as well as the actual beliefs. Our study is ideally suited to measure rational beliefs, i.e. the true average price of discrimination, because we precisely estimate individual marginal products of labor using the team production function. Our design is less suited to directly measure whether decision makers have biased beliefs about the average price of discrimination. The reason is that we make every conceivable effort to implement a natural field experiment to avoid distorted responses from moral bias. Thus, asking participants in NoInfo directly about their

---

[22] Altonji and Pierret (2001: 316) explain that they "are using the term 'statistical discrimination' as synonymous with the term 'rational expectations' in the economics literature. We mean that in the absence of full information, firms distinguish between individuals with different characteristics based on statistical regularities. That is, firms form stereotypes that are rational given their information."

expected price of choosing one candidate over the other is not an option.[23] Instead, we elicit beliefs about the average price of discrimination indirectly, from a sample of similar juveniles. Eliciting beliefs serves two purposes: to test whether the team production is thought to be type-specific (see section A below), and to assess the relative explanatory power of animus-driven and belief-driven prejudice in accounting for observed discrimination in NoInfo (see section B).

A) Eliciting beliefs

We recruit $n = 353$ participants with Danish-sounding and Muslim-sounding names from secondary schools on the outskirts of Copenhagen where we do not recruit for the experiment.[24] We carefully describe the work task to participants and elicit beliefs about the productivity of individuals and teams. In particular, each participant is presented with the names of 7 randomly selected workers and 6 randomly selected teams, all of the same gender as the participant. Participants are asked to guess how many letters each worker packed in round 1 and each team packed in round 2. To benchmark their expectations, we inform participants about the median production in round 1 and round 2 (see appendix H for details). Participants are rewarded for guessing correctly (using a quadratic scoring rule[25]).

Figure 3 shows participants' average beliefs about production in round 1 and 2 by ethnic type of the participant. The horizontal axis shows beliefs about productivity differences *same* minus *other*. The vertical axis shows beliefs about productivity differences between homogeneous teams of the same type as the participant and heterogeneous teams. Each dot represents one participant. The figure shows that the black dots tend to be located slightly to the right and above the zero lines, while white dots tend to be located to the left and below the zero lines. These tendencies reflect the fact that participants of both types correctly tend to think that workers with Danish-sounding names are individually more productive, and that, as a

---

[23] People tend to be more prejudiced than they admit. For example, Kawakami et al. (2009: 277) show "that people's predictions regarding their emotional distress and behavior in response to a racial slur differ drastically from their actual reactions". Studies using survey-based data on animus may therefore yield lower-bound estimates for animus. For example, Charles and Guryan (2008) use 21 survey questions to argue that animus-based prejudice explains up to 25 percent of the racial wage gap in the US.

[24] We omit 42 persons who are classified as having "other" names from the analysis below.

[25] Participants receive $\max(0; 50 - 0.03d^2)$ where d is the difference between the true productivity and the guess. Average earnings in the belief elicitation study are €13.6.

consequence, teams with two workers with Danish-sounding names are more productive than teams with two workers with Muslim-sounding names.

Figure 3: Beliefs about production in round 1 and 2

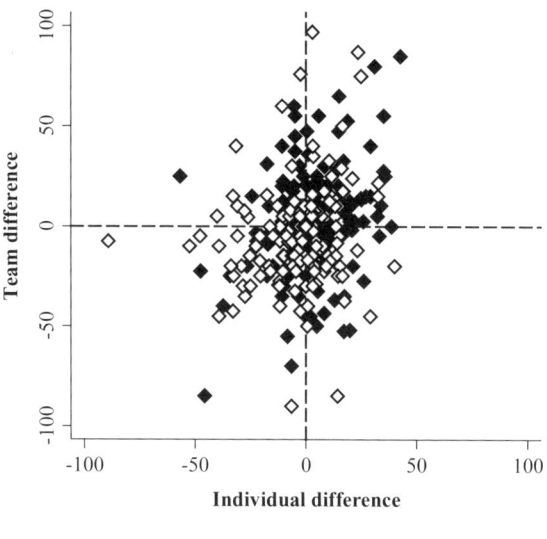

◆ Danish-sounding   ◇ Muslim-sounding

Notes: The horizontal axis shows the difference in average beliefs for numbers of letters packed individually in round 1 by workers of the same ethnic type minus the other ethnic type for participants with Danish-sounding (black dots) and Muslim-sounding names (white dots). The vertical axis shows the difference in average beliefs for number of letters packed in round 2 by homogeneous teams (both workers of the same ethnic type as participant) minus number of letters packed in round 2 by heterogeneous teams for participants with Danish-sounding (black dots) and Muslim sounding names (white dots). $N = 353$, of which 204 participants have Danish-sounding names and 149 have Muslim-sounding names. Two outliers with values > 100 are omitted from the figure.

Statistical testing confirms this visual impression. We find that participants have qualitatively correct beliefs in the sense that they believe that individual workers with Danish-sounding names pack more letters on average than workers with Muslim-sounding names ($p = 0.004$, Wilcoxon signed-rank test, WSR). However, average beliefs are quantitatively biased since the true difference across types of workers is larger than the expected difference (16 vs. 3 letters)[26]. In other words, participants underestimate the true productivity difference across

---

[26] We reject the hypothesis that the median person believes the difference to be equal to the true difference ($p = 0.000$, WSR). This result also holds for each ethnic group separately ($p = 0.000$, WSR).

types. Consistent with the belief that workers with Danish-sounding names are individually more productive, we find that teams with more Danish workers are believed to more productive.

Importantly, we find no evidence for ethnic prejudice in the sense that the team production function is *thought* to be type-specific. Our analysis in table 2 has shown that, after controlling for individual productivity, heterogeneous teams in fact are equally productive as homogeneous teams. The analysis below shows that participants do not think that workers earn more in a homogeneous team than a heterogeneous team, for given round 1 output. Put differently, neither do the juveniles believe nor do they have a reason to believe that selecting a co-worker of the same type is more profitable for given productivities of workers. To test, we regress

$$\Delta_i = \beta_0 + \beta_1 \delta_i + \beta_2 Danish + \varepsilon_i,$$

where Δ_i and δ_i capture the participants' beliefs about output of teams and individuals of different ethnic types. More specifically, Δ_i is participant i's belief about output in a homogenous team of the same type as i minus i's belief about output in a heterogeneous team. Thus, Δ_i captures how much participants with Danish-sounding names thought that all-Danish teams outperform heterogeneous teams, and vice versa for participants with Muslim-sounding names. The variable δ_i is i's belief about output of individual workers of the same type as i minus i's belief about output of workers of the other type. Thus, δ_i captures how much participants with Danish-sounding names thought that Danish workers outperform Muslim workers, and vice versa for participants with Muslim-sounding names. The dummy variable *Danish* equals 1 if the participant has a Danish-sounding name and is used to check whether the two groups differ in their beliefs about the production function.

The regression yields an insignificant coefficient β_0 which suggests that participants do not expect homogeneous and heterogeneous teams to be different, after controlling for beliefs about differences in individual productivity. We find $\beta_1 > 0$ which suggests that differences in beliefs about individual productivity translate into differences in beliefs about team productivity. The estimate for β_2 is not significant indicating that the two groups do not have different beliefs about the type-specificity of the production function, after controlling for beliefs about individual productivity differences. In summary, beliefs about individual productivity differences across types explain differences across homogenous and heterogeneous teams. In addition, homogenous teams are not generally believed to outperform heterogeneous teams, and these beliefs are not different across ethnic type of participant.

B) Animus-driven and belief-driven prejudice matter

We now show that taking prejudice into account substantially improves predictions in NoInfo compared to the benchmark case of accurate statistical discrimination (ASD). We find that ASD predicts discrimination rates inaccurately and that there is a substantial gap between decision makers' predicted earnings according to ASD and observed earnings. Taking the two types of prejudice into account provides much more accurate predictions for discrimination choices and explains the earnings gap almost entirely (97.2%) for one ethnic type and about half (48.5%) of the gap for the other type.

To show that prejudice matters for discrimination, we compare 4 scenarios which differ by assumptions about decision makers' animus and beliefs.

a) No animus, rational beliefs. ASD assumes that decision makers have no animus and maximize expected earnings given rational beliefs about average productivity of ethnic types.[27] Our experiment provides a rare opportunity to test the predictions of ASD because we can retrieve rational beliefs from the distribution of workers' output in phase 1 as follows. For each decision maker *i*, we sample observed round 1 output of two candidates of different types. We estimate the marginal product of labor (MPL) for *i* with either candidate using model A from table 2. Decision maker *i*'s price of choosing one worker over the other is the difference between these MPLs. By repeatedly sampling and averaging, we obtain the expected price for *i* of choosing one type over the other (see Appendix I for details). Because workers with Danish-sounding names are on average more productive than those with Muslim-sounding names in our sample, we find that ASD predicts that all decision makers choose the worker with the Danish-sounding name. However, only about half of decision makers (49%) do so. The

---

[27] While ASD maximizes expected earnings absent precise information about candidates' productivities, it does not yield the first-best outcome. Losses occur when choosing the candidate of the more productive type because decision makers by chance pick a less productive worker when type-productivity distributions overlap. The loss due to limited information is 2.5 percent of round 2 earnings. Yet, there is a clear incentive for ASD in NoInfo. In fact, earnings are 2.5 percent higher with ASD than with random choice of partner.

misprediction is particularly pronounced for decision makers with Muslim-sounding names (only 10.5 percent choose *other*).[28]

b) No animus, biased beliefs. This scenario serves to evaluate the predictive power of statistical discrimination with elicited (i.e. inaccurate) beliefs. We use the same procedure as in a) to retrieve elicited beliefs except that we draw from the distribution of elicited beliefs about round 1 output. We find that statistical discrimination *cum* biased beliefs does not improve predictions compared to ASD. Section A above has shown that elicited beliefs are quantitatively biased in the sense that the true productivity differences across types are underestimated. However, because beliefs were not strongly biased, belief-driven prejudice yields the same predictions as ASD.[29]

c) Animus, rational beliefs. This scenario serves to evaluate the predictive power of animus given rational beliefs. To calculate predictions, we use rational beliefs as described in a) and feed those beliefs into our estimate of taste-based discrimination treatment Info (see model 1 in table 3) to estimate the probability that decision maker *i* chooses *same*. By doing so, we assume that the distribution of animus-driven prejudice is the same in treatment Info and NoInfo. This is assumption is warranted since decision makers were randomly allocated to treatments.

Taking animus-driven prejudice into account improves the prediction for the decision makers with Danish-sounding names from 100 to 79.1 percent. This prediction is not statistically different from the observed 66.7 percent ($p = 0.711$, Fisher exact test).[30] The prediction for the decision makers with Muslim-sounding names is also improved. Now, 57.3 percent (rather than 100 percent) are predicted to choose *other*. Yet, the prediction is still different from the observed 10.5 percent ($p = 0.013$, Fisher exact test).

d) Animus, biased beliefs. In this scenario, we feed elicited beliefs (as described in b above) into our estimate of animus from treatment Info (as described in c above). Note that while

---

[28] The fact that the vast majority (89.5 percent) of decision makers with Muslim-sounding names chooses *same* in NoInfo suggests that any preference for a weekday that may have been present is swamped by ethnic preferences in our sample. Recall from section 3 that our randomized matching procedure guarantees that candidates are randomly allocated to weekdays.

[29] Note that this is the case in our experiment because discrimination choices are discrete. Had discrimination involved a continuous variable like wages, any bias in expected MPL would translate into a cost.

[30] Tests in this section assume an equal number of observations for predicted and observed discrimination rates.

biased beliefs do not make a difference for predictions given that decision makers have no animus in our design, they do make a difference given animus-driven prejudice. The reason is that the prediction moves discretely with beliefs absent animus (all choose the type believed to be more productive on average) but moves continuously in the presence of animus (the demand for discrimination is smooth, see figure 2).

We find that taking both types of prejudice into account further improves the predictions. The prediction is now perfectly accurate for decision makers with Danish-sounding names (67.3 vs. 66.7 percent observed).[31] The prediction also improves for decision makers with Muslim-sounding names, but there is still a some discrepancy (60.8 vs. 89.5 percent). However, the predicted and observed discrimination rates are not significantly different after accounting for prejudice ($p = 0.232$, Fisher exact test).

Table 4 shows how the gap between earnings with ASD and observed earnings can be explained by prejudice using the scenarios described above. The table shows earnings foregone to decision makers by deviating from ASD, in percent of decision makers' round 2 earnings with ASD. The total gap is 3.6 percent (or about €2.3 per decision maker). The gap is smaller for decision makers with Danish-sounding names (1.6 vs. 5.8 percent) because they tend to choose the Danish-sounding, i.e. on average more productive, candidate more often.

The top row of table 4 shows that statistical discrimination *cum* biased beliefs (scenario b) cannot account for the earnings gap. The second row shows the explanatory power of scenario c. We find that animus *cum* rational beliefs predicts a loss of 1.7 percent relative to ASD. Note that the predictions are rather different for the two ethnic types. Decision makers with Muslim-sounding names have higher losses (2.3 vs. 1.1 percent). The main reason for this difference is that our estimate of animus predicts that decision makers of either type choose *same* more often than *other*. Hence, decision makers with Danish-sounding names tend to choose the more productive type more often than the decision makers with Muslim-sounding names. Assuming animus *cum* rational expectations explains about 40 percent (= 2.3/5.8) and two thirds (= 1.1/1.6) of the gap for Danish-sounding and Muslim-sounding decision makers, respectively.

---

[31] This highly precise prediction is remarkable given its out-of-sample nature. Recall that the demand for taste-based discrimination is estimated by forcing all cost to be positive in Info while the (average) cost of discrimination is negative for decision makers with Danish-sounding names in NoInfo.

Table 4: Earnings foregone relative to earnings with accurate statistical discrimination (ASD)

Type of prejudice	Belief	Animus	Earnings foregone (percent)		
			Danish-sounding	Muslim-sounding	Overall
Belief-driven	Elicited	None	0.0	0.0	0.0
Animus-driven	Rational	Elicited	-1.1	-2.3	-1.7
Both	Elicited	Elicited	-1.5	-2.8	-2.2
Observed	-	-	-1.6	-5.8	-3.6

Notes: The table shows earnings foregone relative to the benchmark of accurate statistical discrimination in percent of decision makers' round 2 earnings. Rational beliefs are retrieved for each decision maker i by repeatedly sampling from candidates' observed round 1 output. We then estimate the marginal product of labor (MPL) using model A in table 2 for each draw. Elicited beliefs are retrieved analogously by drawing from elicited beliefs (see section 4.3). In row 1, i chooses the candidate of the type with the higher average MPL given elicited beliefs. In rows 2 and 3, we estimate probabilities of choosing *same* from model 1 in table 3 and using the average price according to rational or elicited beliefs, respectively. We use these probabilities to calculate a weighted average of earnings for either type.

The third row of table 4 shows the explanatory power of scenario d. We find that the loss predicted by both types of prejudice is about 2.2 percent of earnings in the benchmark case.[32] Note that biased beliefs do matter given animus (about half a percentage point). Thus, adding biased beliefs to animus-driven prejudice explains an additional 14 to 33 percent of the gap.

In summary, we find that accurate statistical discrimination (ASD) cannot explain observed outcomes. We find that both types of prejudice together explain about 60 percent of the gap between earnings with ASD and observed earnings. The gap is almost perfectly (97.2 percent) explained for decision makers with Danish-sounding names. For decision makers with

---

[32] Note that earnings foregone in NoInfo refer to all decision makers. In contrast, the earnings foregone reported in Info (8.4 percent) refer to the average discriminator. The comparable number for all decision makers is a loss of 2.8 percent. The difference (2.8 vs. 2.2) is mainly due to the fact that the price of choosing *same* was much smaller in NoInfo than in Info (averages are 1.1 vs. 9.8 percent). This is the case for two reasons. First, the price is positive by design in Info while it is positive or negative in NoInfo, depending on the type of decision maker. Second, in NoInfo the average price is relevant for choices while in Info it is the realization of a random draw, and some of these have high values. A decision maker with a strong animus discriminates in both treatments, but the implied price paid for this animus-driven prejudice is lower in NoInfo than Info.

Muslim-sounding names, prejudice provides a much better prediction than ASD (48.2 percent of the gap is explained), but a considerable unexplained gap remains.[33]

5 Concluding remarks

This study develops a novel experimental approach to measuring the price of ethnic prejudice paid by discriminators in the work place. We show that part of this price is paid deliberately and is due to animus, and part of the price is paid unintentionally and is due to biased beliefs.

We find that statistical discrimination along with rational expectations (i.e. accurate statistical discrimination) grossly mispredicts observed behavior. Compared to this benchmark, decision makers leave about 4 percent of earnings on the table. We show that about 60 percent of this earnings gap can be accounted for by animus and belief-driven prejudice. We isolate taste-based discrimination by controlling for beliefs, i.e. by informing decision makers about the true productivity of job candidates, and by randomly assigning a price of discrimination to decision makers. Using a sample from Denmark, we find that discrimination is common even at a substantial price, that majority and minority groups are equally likely to discriminate for given prices, and that the demand for discrimination is remarkably elastic. Our best estimate is that the probability to discriminate falls by about 9 percent if the price of discrimination goes up by 10 percent. We use this estimate together with elicited beliefs to evaluate the predictive power of animus-driven and belief-driven prejudice.

Below, we discuss three potential sources of mismeasurement of prejudice due to selection effects and conclude that selection is not likely to have caused bias in one way or another. Finally, we emphasize that our quantitative findings should not be extrapolated to employment decisions in large firms without further consideration because incentives for personnel managers may be opaque or differ substantially from the sharp and controlled incentives for decision makers in our experiment.

First, we may underestimate animus in the general population because our sample is not representative of the Danish population. We recruit juveniles from secondary schools in

---

[33] We can only speculate what may explain the remaining gap. A possibility is "implicit discrimination" (Bertrand et al. 2005). However, it is not entirely clear why implicit discrimination should be more important for minority than for majority decision makers.

Copenhagen who have very similar age and education and are all fluent in the majority language. Such relatively well-educated and integrated juveniles as a group may have systematically lower animus than the average Dane or Muslim living in Denmark. In fact, available research suggests that (voiced) animus decreases with education and income but increases with age (e.g. Charles and Guryan 2008).

Second, we may over- or underestimate differences in animus across ethnic types. We find that minority and majority groups are equally likely to discriminate for a given price. This result is surprising in the light of evidence suggesting that minorities have more pronounced "homophily" (in the diction of Curarrini et al. 2009) than majorities. We may underestimate the difference due to unobserved heterogeneity in income in our sample. While the evidence presented in Charles and Guryan (2008) suggests that animus decreases with income, taste-based discrimination may well also increase with income (if it is a "normal" good). However, we may overestimate the difference due to a subtle name-related selection effect. A juvenile is classified as having a Muslim-sounding name in our experiment if his parents chose such a name, but is classified as having a Danish-sounding (or other) name if they did not. If the name choice by parents is correlated with animus, we would tend to overestimate differences in animus across ethnic groups. However, this effect seems to be of minor relevance since we find no difference in animus across ethnic types.

Third, we may over- or underestimate the relevance of belief-driven prejudice. We elicit beliefs on a different sample of juveniles and argue that elicited beliefs are a precise proxy of decision makers' beliefs in NoInfo. This claim seems plausible because both groups are similar in observables, both groups have an incentive to form beliefs, and, perhaps most importantly, we find that elicited beliefs provide a more precise prediction (given animus) of observed behavior than rational beliefs. Yet, elicited beliefs may be more or less accurate than decision makers' beliefs in NoInfo. On the one hand, beliefs may be less accurate because participants in the elicitation study are not experienced in the work task. On the other hand, elicited beliefs may be more accurate because participants were given explicit incentives for guessing correctly and may have thought more explicitly about how others perform.

A remarkable side result of our study is that, after controlling for individual productivity differences, minority and majority workers are equally productive in teamwork whether they work with someone from the same or the other ethnic type. In addition, we find no evidence for the claim that majority workers think they cannot work equally well with a minority worker than with a majority worker, all else equal. Thus, this type of belief-based prejudice about teamwork receives no support in our study. However, we do find evidence for a different type of belief-based prejudice. We find that participants of both types underestimate the remarkably pronounced differences in productivity across types. Thus, we find that both majority and minority types seem, perhaps surprisingly, to expect less of a difference in productivity that there in fact is.

The extent to which the quantitative estimates from our experiment extrapolate to hiring choices, in particular in large firms, must remain an open issue for two reasons. First, we may over- or underestimate the importance of belief-driven prejudice compared to personnel managers who may have more or less accurate beliefs than decision makers our sample. On the one hand, personnel managers in large firms may be able to draw on extensive internal statistics and therefore have more accurate beliefs about the average productivity by ethnic type than decision makers in NoInfo. On the other hand, the work task in our experiment was well-defined and simple compared to collaborative tasks in large firms. It is therefore relatively easy for our decision makers to predict productivity accurately. Second, we may over- or underestimate the sensitivity of taste-based discrimination to the price of prejudice because decision makers (in Info) faced a clear and known price for discrimination while incentives may be opaque or weak for a personnel officer in a large firm. Decision makers in our experiment are directly affected (monetarily and non-monetarily) by their choices because they make a consequential choice of whom to work with in a team. In contrast, personnel managers do not necessarily physically work with new hires and may also be largely shielded from monetary consequences of their choices. On the other hand, large corporations may have particular policies (like affirmative action programs) on discrimination in place which may provide incentives against discrimination.

In conclusion, our results suggest that belief-driven and animus-driven ethnic prejudice are important causes of ethnic discrimination in the workplace, and need to be taken into account above and beyond the theory of accurate statistical discrimination.

References

Altonji, J.G. and Blank, R. (1999): Race and Gender in the Labor Market. *Handbook of Labor Economics* 3(13): 3143-3259.

Altonji, J.G. and Pierret, C.R. (2001): Employer Learning and Statistical Discrimination. *Quarterly Journal of Economics* 116(1): 313-50.

Anderson, L.R., Fryer, R.G. and Holt, C.A. (2006): Discrimination: Experimental Evidence from Psychology and Economics, in: W.M. Rodgers (ed.): *Handbook on the Economics of Discrimination*. Cheltenham: Edward Elgar, 97-115.

Arrow, K.J. (1973): The Theory of Discrimination. In: O. Ashenfelter and A. Rees (eds.): *Discrimination in Labor Markets*. Princeton, N.J., Princeton University Press.

Ayres, I. and Siegelman, P. (1995): Race and Gender Discrimination in Bargaining for a New Car. *American Economic Review* 85(3): 304–321.

Baccara, M., Collard-Wexler, A., Felli, L. and Yariv, L. (2009): Gender and Racial Biases: Evidence from Child Adoption. Working paper NYU.

Becker, G.S. (1957): *The Economics of Discrimination*. University of Chicago Press.

Bertrand, M., Chugh, D. and Mullainathan, S. (2005): Implicit Discrimination. *American Economic Review* 95(2): 94-98.

Bertrand, M. and Mullainathan, S. (2004): Are Emily and Greg More Employable than Lakisha and Jamal? A Field Experiment on Labor Market Discrimination. *American Economic Review* 94(4): 991-1013.

Carlsson, M. and Rooth, D.O. (2007): Evidence of Ethnic Discrimination in the Swedish Labor Market Using Experimental Data. *Labour Economics* 14: 716-729.

Caruso, E.M., Rahnev, D.A. and Banaji, M.R. (2009): Using Conjoint Analysis to Detect Discrimination: Revealing Covert Preferences from Overt Choices. *Social Cognition* 27(1): 128-37.

Charles, K.K. and Guryan, J. (2008): Prejudice and Wages: An Empirical Assessment of Becker's "The Economics of Discrimination". *Journal of Political Economy* 166(5): 773-809.

Currarini, S., Jackson, M.O. and Pin, P. (2009): An Economic Model of Friendship: Homophily, Minorities, and Segregation. *Econometrica* 77(4): 1003-1045.

Daniel, W. (1968): *Racial Discrimination in England*, Middlesex: Penguin Books.

Fershtman, C. and Gneezy, U. (2001): Discrimination in a Segmented Society: An Experimental Approach. *Quarterly Journal of Economics* 116(1): 351-77.

Goldin, C. and Rouse, C. (2000): Orchestrating Impartiality: The Impact of "Blind" Auditions on Female Musicians. *American Economic Review* 90(4): 715-741.

Hamermesh, D.S. and Biddle, J.E. (1994): Beauty and the Labor Market. *American Economic Review* 84(5): 1174-94.

Heckman, J.J. (1998): Detecting Discrimination. *Journal of Economic Perspectives* 12(2): 101-116.

Heckman, J.J. and Siegelman, P. (1993): The Urban Institute Audit Studies: Their Methods and Findings. In M. Fix and R. Struyk, eds. *Clear and Convincing Evidence: Measurement of Discrimination in America*, 187-258.

Holm, H.J. (2001): What's in a Name? An Ethnical Discrimination Experiment. Working paper, Lund University.

Jowell, R. and Prescott-Clarke, P. (1970): Racial Discrimination and White-collar Workers in Britain. *Race* 11: 397-417.

Kawakami, K., Dunn, E., Karmali, F. and Dovidio, J.F. (2009): Mispredicting Affective and Behavioral Responses to Racism. *Science* 323: 276-278.

Lang, K. (1986): A Language Theory of Discrimination. *Quarterly Journal of Economics* 101(2): 363-382.

Levitt, S. (2004): Testing Theories of Discrimination: Evidence from Weakest Link. *Journal of Law and Economics* 47: 431-452.

List, J. (2004): The Nature and Extent of Discrimination in the Marketplace: Evidence from the Field. *Quarterly Journal of Economics* 119(1): 49-89.

List, J. (2006): Field Experiments: A Bridge Between Lab and Naturally Occurring Data. *Advances in Economic Analysis and Policy* 6(2): Article 8.

Möbius, M.M. and Rosenblat, T.S. (2006): Why Beauty Matters. *American Economic Review* 96(1): 222-235.

Neumark, D. (2010): Detecting Discrimination in Audit and Correspondence Studies. NBER working paper 16448.

Neumark, D., Bank, R.J. and van Nort, K.D. (1996): Sex Discrimination in Restaurant Hiring: an Audit Study. *Quarterly Journal of Economics* 111(3): 915-941.

Oreopoulos, P. (2009): Why Do Skilled Immigrants Struggle in the Labor Market? A Field Experiment with Six Thousand Resumes. NBER Working Paper 15036.

Pager, D. (2007): The Use of Field Experiments for Studies of Employment Discrimination: Contributions, Critiques, and Directions for the Future. *Annals of the American Academy of Political and Social Science* 609: 104-133.

Pager, D., Western, B. and Bonikowski, B. (2009): Discrimination in a Low-Wage Labor Market. *American Sociological Review* 74(5): 777-799.

Phelps, E. (1972): The Statistical Theory of Racism and Sexism. *American Economic Review* 62(4): 659-661.

Pope, D.G. and Sydnor, J.R. (2011): What's in a Picture? Evidence of Discrimination from Prosper.com. *Journal of Human Resources* 46(1): 53-92.

Riach, P.A. and Rich, J. (2002): Field Experiments of Discrimination in the Market Place. *Economic Journal* 112(483): 480-518.

Yinger, J. (1998): Evidence on Discrimination in Consumer Markets. *Journal of Economic Perspectives* 12(2): 23-40.

Zizzo, D. (2010): Experimenter Demand Effects in Economic Experiments. *Experimental Economics* 13(1): 75-98.

Appendices

Appendix A: Flyer used for recruiting

Appendix B: Location and participants
      Figure B1: Location of schools from which participants were recruited
      Figure B2: The control room
      Figure B3: Floor plan

Appendix C: Description of the work task
      Figure C1: Photograph of a workstation

Appendix D: Validation of classification of first names
      Table D1: Effectiveness of first names as marker of ethnic type

Appendix E: Using productivity differences as proxy for the price of discrimination
      Table E1: The demand for discrimination using output differences as a proxy for *Price*

Appendix F: Robustness of price effect with respect to the decision maker's productivity
      Table F1: Discrimination and the decision maker's productivity

Appendix G: Testing for random assignment of price (simulation)

Appendix H: Eliciting productivity beliefs
      Table H1: Average output guesses by participants in complementary study

Appendix I: Decomposition of the earnings gap

Appendix A: Flyer used for recruiting

Tjen penge!

Har du lyst til at tjene ekstra penge?

Københavns Universitet skal sende 40.000 invitationer til vores nye internet platform (www.econ.ku.dk/iLEE), og vi har brug for hjælp til at pakke brevene.

Du skal kunne arbejde 2 gange 2 timer. De første 2 timer skal være i uge 49 (3. - 7. dec.), og de sidste 2 timer i uge 50/51 (10. - 19. dec.). Arbejdet foregår i centrum af København og vi tilbyder en god løn.

Arbejdstiden vil kunne være hverdage mellem kl. 13 og kl. 21. Jo mere fleksibel du er, desto større chance er der, for at vi kan bruge dig. Vi aftaler naturligvis det specifikke tidspunkt i god tid inden arbejdet.

Du vil blive aflønnet efter, hvor mange breve du pakker, og vi forventer i gennemsnit at betale cirka 180 kr./time.

Hvis du er interesseret så ring på tlf. 35 32 44 04 / 35 32 30 59 mellem klokken 10 og 18 eller send en e-mail med navn og telefonnummer til iLEE@econ.ku.dk.

KØBENHAVNS UNIVERSITET

Translation: Earn money! Would you like to earn some extra money? The University of Copenhagen has to mail 40'000 invitation letters for a new internet platform, and we are looking for help to pack these letters.
You are supposed to work twice for 2 hours. The first 2 hours are in week 49 ... the second in week 50/51.
Work is to be done in the city center and we pay a good salary. Work times are between 1 p.m. and 9 p.m. You are more likely to be hired if you are more flexible with respect to work times. We will of course make a specific agreement with sufficient notice.
You will be paid according to how many letters you pack and we expect to pay about 180 kr. (about €24) per hour.
Call us on …between .. and .. or send an e-mail with your name on phone number to … if you are interested.

Appendix B: Location and participants

Figure B1 shows the secondary schools from which participants were recruited for the experiment (red symbols), for the belief elicitation and name validation studies (blue symbols) and the pre-test (purple marker in the lower left corner). The flag indicates the location of the University premises where work was carried out.

Figure B1: Location of schools from which participants were recruited [34]

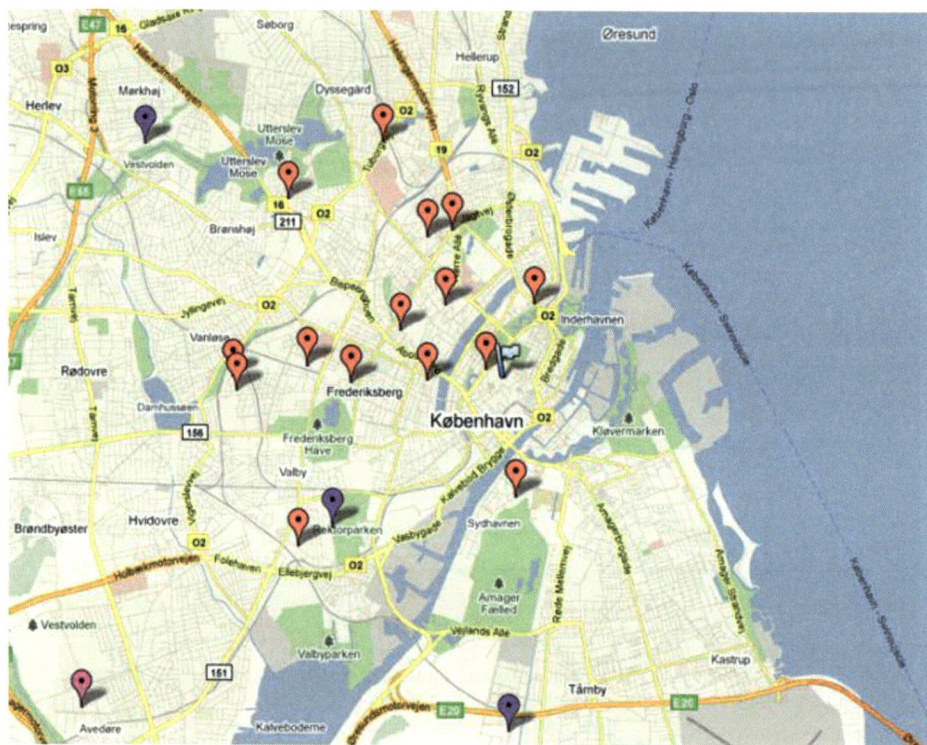

---

[34] The figure has more than eleven red markers as some of the schools where we recruited for the experiment have several campuses in Copenhagen.

Figure B2: The control room

Figure B3: Floor plan

The University of Copenhagen generously provided us with an entire floor (app. 320 m^2) of 11 offices which were furnished with tables and chairs. Two offices were used for storage of materials, one office was used as control room (see figure B2) and work was carried out in the remaining eight offices.

Appendix C: Description of the work task

The participants were seated in a two-person office at a workstation facing the wall. Figure C1 shows a photograph of the workstation.

Figure C1: Photograph of a workstation

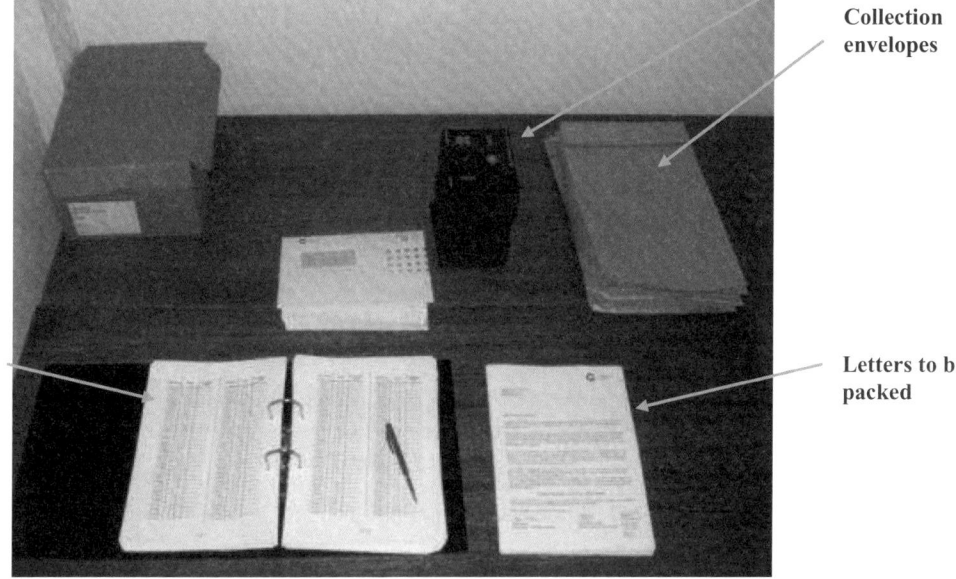

Each letter had a an ID number (ranging from 12,000 to 51,999). The order of the letters was randomized so each participant could have letters from the entire interval.

The 40,000 letters had to be sorted into 5 main categories (A to E). These were then split further into a total of 96 subcategories (A-1 to E-96). The sub-categories were assigned randomly and were not printed on the letters. Each participant would get letters belonging to six subcategories and would have to sort the letters accordingly.

For each letter, the task was to: Look up the letter's ID number in a binder with 600 pages and see which category (A-1 to E-96) the letter belongs to; Look up the category type (A to E) in a separate list and see whether the letter should include a gift (letters in categories B and D should include a small foam puzzle) ; Fold the letter and stuff it into an envelope. If category B or D, then also include a gift ; Close the envelope ; Sort the envelope into the collection envelope with the subcategory label written on the outside.

The participants received both oral and written instructions on how to do the task. These instructions were given individually and we demonstrate how to pack a letter. The participant then packed a under supervision to verify understanding of the procedure. If successful, the participants worked alone for 90 minutes. An alarm clock was set in the control room to enforce to time limit. After the 90 minutes, we stopped the participants and counted the number of letters packed. In total, the participants spend less than two hours at the University in each round.

Appendix D: Validation of classification of first names

As in correspondence tests, we use names as a marker of ethnicity. However, we do not use fictitious and highly stereotypical names but the actual names of workers. We categorize these names into ethnic types using our judgment complemented by lists of "typical" Danish and Muslim names we found on the web (such as www.muslimbabynames.net).

To test if actual names are effective markers of ethnicity, we run a complementary study with $n = 144$ juveniles in a secondary school on the outskirts of Copenhagen where we do not recruit for the experiment. The questionnaire (available from the authors on request) presents respondents with 4 randomly drawn pairs of candidates (i.e. using the actual names and actual pairs decision makers faced) and asks them classify the names as either Danish or Muslim. More specifically, respondents have the option to classify either, both or none of the two names as 'Danish' or 'Arab/Muslim'. We randomize the order of names for a given choice in any given pair. This task is presented to respondents as part of a "classification study" which also contains 9 other, unrelated, tasks (e.g. classify cities as German or French). Participants are paid a flat fee of DKK 100 (€13.3) for completing the survey.

Table D1: Effectiveness of first names as marker of ethnic type

	Boys		Girls		
Concordance	Danish-sounding	Muslim-sounding	Danish-sounding	Muslim-sounding	*Overall*
Danish names	80%	87%	84%	94%	*83%*
Muslim names	97%	94%	86%	92%	*92%*
Overall	*89%*	*90%*	*85%*	*93%*	*88%*
Confound					
Danish names	2%	3%	3%	5%	*2%*
Muslim names	0%	0%	1%	0%	*1%*
Overall	*1%*	*2%*	*2%*	*3%*	*1%*

Notes: The table shows the percentage (over of all names and respondents) of classifications in the survey study that are in line ("concordance") or conflict ("confound") with the classification into ethnic types in the experiment. Concordance occurs, for example, if a name we classify as Danish-sounding in the experiment is classified by respondents as Danish-sounding. Confound occurs, for example, if a name we classify as Danish-sounding is classified by respondents as Muslim-sounding. The number of respondents is $n = 144$.

Table D1 shows that concordance rates are very high and confound is rare. In particular, the last column shows that 83 percent of the names we classify as Danish-sounding and 92 percent of those we classify as Muslim-sounding are categorized by respondents in concordance with our classification. Importantly, it very rarely happens (1 percent of the cases) that names we classify as belonging to one ethnic type are classified as belonging to the other category by respondents. Concordance and confound rates are similar for respondents with Danish-sounding and Muslim-sounding names.

Appendix E: Using productivity differences as proxy for the price of discrimination

This appendix shows that our main result in Info (that an increase in price causally reduces taste-based discrimination) is robust to using a different type of team production function to estimate prices.

In section 4.1, we estimate the price from the marginal productivity of labor obtained from a particular type team production function (model A in table 3). We then use these (randomly assigned) prices to estimate the demand for discrimination (and the willingness to pay). By doing so, we assume that the price, and implicitly also the team production function, is known to decision makers. To demonstrate robustness, we use "raw" round 1 output differences as a proxy for the price in the estimation of the demand for discrimination and therefore tie the price of prejudice directly to observables. We find very similar results either way.

Table E1 replicates the analysis in table 3 using (half of) the difference of round 1 output between the candidates as a proxy for the price of discrimination. The coefficient of $\Delta Prod_{jk}$ in model (8) shows that if price goes up by €1, decision makers are about 3 percent less likely to discriminate. This estimate is similar to our result for *Price* in table 3 (3.0 vs. 3.6 percent). Also note that models (9) to (11) yield very similar results as models (2) to (4) in table 3.

Table E1: The demand for discrimination using output differences as a proxy for *Price*

Dependent variable: Discr	(8)	(9)	(10)	(11)
ΔProd	-0.030**	-0.029**	-0.028**	-0.029*
	(0.013)	(0.014)	(0.014)	(0.016)
Danish-sounding		0.014		0.088
		(0.160)		(0.273)
Male		-0.063		-0.138
		(0.152)		(0.266)
Danish-sounding * ΔProd			-0.001	-0.010
			(0.020)	(0.035)
Male * ΔProd			-0.005	0.010
			(0.017)	(0.029)
N	37	37	37	37
Adj. R^2	0.073	0.076	0.074	0.079

Notes: The table shows average marginal effects for probit regressions. Numbers in parentheses are robust standard errors. The dependent variable *Discr* = 1 for a discriminator and 0 otherwise. The variable $\Delta Prod_{jk}$ is the difference in output in round 1 by *other* minus output by *same*. To make the numbers comparable, we multiply the difference by 0.5 as the joint output was split among the two team members and express values in Euros, i.e. multiply with €0.5 per letter packed. *Danish-sounding* and *Male* are dummy variables characterizing decision maker *i*. * $p < 0.10$, ** $p < 0.05$, *** $p < 0.01$

Appendix F: Robustness of price effect with respect to the decision maker's productivity

Our discussion of the response of taste-based discrimination to the price of prejudice in Info in section 4.1 is entirely cast in terms of earnings foregone by choosing one candidate over the other, i.e. is based on opportunity cost. Below, we address issues relating to the absolute and relative productivity of the decision maker.

Table F1 investigates if decision makers with high productivity in round 1 tend to be less likely to discriminate. Such an effect is plausible if those with a strong preference for money work hard and also tend to choose a co-worker primarily on the basis of monetary concerns. But we find that the effect is weak is best ($Prod_1$ is insignificant in models 5 and 6). The table also serves to investigate whether the decision maker's productivity in round 1 relative to the productivities of the two candidates biases our estimates of the demand for discrimination. Our conclusion from the discussion below is that it does not.

Table F1: Discrimination and the decision maker's productivity

Dependent variable: Discr	(5)	(6)	(7)
Price	-0.030*	-0.030**	-0.017
	(0.016)	(0.015)	(0.018)
$Prod_1$	-0.046*	-0.044	-0.043
	(0.026)	(0.033)	(0.032)
$Prod_1^2$	0.000	0.000	0.000
	(0.000)	(0.000)	(0.000)
Abs. distance to *same*		0.001	-0.003
		(0.008)	(0.007)
Same candidate below			-0.153
			(0.199)
Both candidates below			0.101
			(0.268)
N	37	37	37
R^2	0.147	0.147	0.177

Notes: The table shows average marginal effects estimated from Probit regressions. Numbers in parentheses are robust standard errors. The dependent variable *Discr* = 1 for a discriminator and 0 otherwise. The variable *Price* is expressed in Euros. $Prod_1$ and $Prod_1^2$ are decision maker i's productivity and its square in round 1. Abs. distance to "same" is the absolute difference in round 1 productivity between decision maker i and the candidate of the same ethnic type as i. "*Same*" *candidate below* is a dummy variable taking the value 1 if the productivity of the decision maker in round 1 is between the two candidates. *Both candidates below* is a dummy variable taking the value 1 if the productivity of the decision maker in round 1 is higher than that of both candidates. * $p < 0.10$, ** $p < 0.05$, *** $p < 0.01$

A potential concern with using an opportunity cost concept is that it does not take relative standing into account. Due to random matching of decision makers into triples, decision makers have a choice between candidates who can be more or less similar to the decision maker in terms of round 1 productivity. A particular concern is that choosing *same* may not reflect a preference for an ethnic type, but a preference for a co-worker with similar productivity. For example, a decision maker may choose *same* to avoid peer pressure and feeling uncomfortable when working with a much more productive co-worker. Model (6) in table F1 includes a variable *Abs. distance to "same"* which measures the absolute productivity difference between the decision maker and the candidate of the same ethnic type. The insignificant coefficient suggests that this concern does not affect the choice of co-worker.[35]

Model (7) in table F1 investigates a potential confound of loss aversion and taste-based discrimination. Due to the randomness of our matching procedure, decision makers have a choice between a) two candidates which are both less productive, b) both more productive, or c) a more and a less productive candidate. Compared to the case of being in a team with a co-worker with the same productivity, discrimination in case a) means incurring an additional loss, in b) foregoing an additional gain, and in c) incurring a loss rather than making a gain. Thus, loss aversion predicts that choosing *same* is less likely in case c) than in a) or b), and less likely in a) than b) for a given price of discrimination. To test, we add *"Same" candidate below* (equal to 1 in case c) and *Both candidates below* (a dummy equal to 1 in case a). The insignificant estimates suggest that loss aversion does not seem to have affected the choice of a co-worker. However, this result should be taken with a grain of salt due to multi-collinearity and the large number of explanatory variables compared to the number of observations.

---

[35] We also find that decision makers do not have a bias in favor of the candidate with more "similar" productivity in a simple non-parametric test. Out of 37 decision makers, 21 choose the "closer", 16 the "further" candidate. This split is not statistically different from a 50:50 split ($p = .560$, χ^2 test).

Appendix G: Testing for random assignment of price (simulation)

A precondition for identifying the causal effect of prices on discrimination choices in treatment Info is that the price of discrimination (i.e. the opportunity cost choosing *same* over *other*) is randomly assigned to decision makers. In particular, the distribution of animus and the distribution of the prices must be independent.

Our matching procedure (see section 3) is sequential and matches (randomly drawn) decision makers with candidates from a pool of suitable candidates. That is, once a decision maker is determined, the candidates are drawn from a constrained set (e.g. the candidates and the decision maker have to be available on the same days). A possible concern is that our matching procedure caused selection in the sense that characteristics of the decision maker constrain the set of set of suitable candidates in such a way that the resulting distribution of prices is not random and independent of decision makers' animus.

Below, we provide three tests for random assignment of prices to decision makers. The tests do not reject the hypothesis of random assignment.

First, we test if the distribution of prices observed in our experiment is normal. Unconstrained random drawing of pairs of candidates implies that the distribution of $Price_i$ follows (half a) normal distribution. Because $Price_i$ is positive by design in Info, we mirror the experimental distribution on 0, and test this distribution for normality using standard tests. We cannot reject the normality assumption ($p = 0.818$, Shapiro-Wilk; $p = 0.721$, Shapiro-Francia; $p = 0.901$, Skewness/Kurtosis test for normality).

Second, we test if the sequentiality of our matching procedure caused a bias in the distribution of productivity differences between candidates. We test for productivity differences because these are directly observable and are a good proxy to $Price_i$ (see appendix E for a discussion). In particular, we test if the observed distribution of productivity differences is different from a simulated distribution which is obtained from random draws without (unintended) constraints. The simulated productivity differences are obtained by sampling from all participants who complete round 1 ($n = 162$) with two constraints which are intended consequences of our design (rather than unintended consequences of sequential sampling). Our simulation imposes that a decision maker is always matched with candidates of the same gender (to avoid confound of gender and ethnicity) and that *same* is by design less productive than *other* (to make choices informative). We sample 1'000 productivity differences for each type of decision maker. From this pool, we randomly draw 37 productivity differences and test the resulting distribution against the experimentally observed distribution using Mann-Whitney (MW) and Kolmogorov-Smirnov (KS) tests. We repeat the draw and run the tests 1'000 times. At a level of significance α, we expect fewer than α percent of these tests to reject (i.e. to have a p-value $< α$) if the null is true. At $α = 0.05$, we find that these tests reject in less than 1 percent of the cases (MW: 0.009, KS: 0.005). At $α = 0.1$, we find that the tests reject in less than 3 percent of the cases (MW: 0.029, KS: 0.009). In summary, our sequential matching procedure yields productivity differences which are indistinguishable from purely random draws of candidates and the sequential matching we use does therefore not seem to bias prices.

Third, we test for the independence of the distribution of animus and the distribution of prices by means of a simulation. This is a joint test for independence and other assumptions which are simultaneously imposed in the simulation. In particular, the simulation imposes a normal distribution of prices, a normal distribution of animus (an assumption we make in using probit regressions), and independence of the two distributions. We also impose utility maximization in that the decision maker discriminates if and only if $a_i \geq Price_i$, just as we do in our estimations (see section 4.2). We compare the simulated distributions to the observed distribution in the experiment using non-parametric tests. We find that our experimental observation is likely to come from a population in which the assumptions above, including independence, jointly hold.

We proceed as follows. We randomly sample $n = 37$ pairs of $Price_i$ and a_i. $Price_i$ is drawn from the best fit of a normal distribution to estimated prices and a_i is drawn from the estimated distribution as explained in section 4.2B. If $a_i \geq Price_i$, we assign a value of $Discr_i = 1$, and $= 0$ otherwise. We calculate the conditional distribution of price for discriminators ($Discr_i = 1$) and non-discriminators, and the share of discriminators. We test these 3 distributions against the respective distributions as observed in the experiment using non-parametric tests. We repeat 1000 times for each distribution and expect a share of less than α (the significance level) of these tests to have p-values $< \alpha$ if the null hypothesis is true.

For the conditional distribution of the price of discriminators we find no significant difference between simulated and observed data. At $\alpha = 0.05$, we find that non-parametric tests reject in less than 3 percent of the cases (Mann-Whitney (MW): 0.024, Kolmogorov-Smirnov (KS): 0.020). At $\alpha = 0.1$, we find that the tests reject in 5 percent or less of the cases (MW: 0.050, KS: 0.040).

For the conditional distribution of the price of non-discriminators we find no significant difference between simulated and observed data. At $\alpha = 0.05$, we find that non-parametric tests reject in less than 2 percent of the cases (MW: 0.011, KS: 0.010). At $\alpha = 0.1$, the tests reject in 3 percent of the cases (MW: 0.030, KS: 0.030).

We find a mean simulated discrimination rate of 38.4 percent (observed is 37.8 percent, $n = 37$). We run 1'000 Chi-square tests to test for differences in the simulated and observed discrimination rate. At $\alpha = 0.05$, we find that the tests reject in less than 1 percent of the cases (χ^2: 0.007), at $\alpha = 0.1$, the tests reject in less than 2 percent of the cases (χ^2: 0.013).

In conclusion, the tests for the conditional prices of discriminators, of non-discriminators and the discrimination rates reveal that the observed data in our experiment does not look different from simulated data imposing random allocation of prices to decision makers.

Appendix H: Eliciting productivity beliefs

We recruit $n = 353$ juveniles to elicit beliefs about individual and team output across ethnic types in the letter packing task from two secondary schools where we do not recruit for the experiment. We carefully explain the work task to these participants and ask them to guess the productivity of actual workers in our experiment. We provide incentives for guessing correctly (the full questionnaire is available from the authors on request).

In particular, we present participants with a table of 7 randomly selected workers of the same gender and ask them to guess how many letters each worker packed when working in isolation in round 1. We also ask them to guess round 2 output for 6 randomly selected teams (2 homogeneous Danish-sounding, 2 homogeneous Muslim-sounding and 2 heterogeneous teams). As a point of reference, we provide participants with the observed median production in rounds 1 and 2. In total, 204 juveniles with Danish-sounding and 149 with Muslim-sounding names participate (42 have names that are classified as "other" and are omitted from the study). Beliefs are incentivized using a quadratic scoring rule. Average earnings are €13.6.

Table H1 shows that both types of participants tend to believe that workers with Danish-sounding names are more productive than workers with Muslim-sounding names when working alone (109 vs. 106 and 101 vs. 98, respectively). Remarkably, these beliefs about individual productivity differences across ethnic types are qualitatively in line with our results for round 1 production (116 vs. 100). However, both types of participants underestimate the true difference across ethnic types (3 vs. 16 letters).

Concerning team output, table H1 shows that both groups expect homogeneous Danish-sounding teams to be more productive than productive than heterogeneous teams which, in turn, are believed to be more productive homogeneous Muslim-sounding teams. The differences in beliefs about team production almost perfectly reflect the differences in beliefs about individual production. In particular, expected output increases by 3 letters by replacing a team worker with a Muslim-sounding name by one with a Danish-sounding name. Note that this almost perfect correspondence holds for participants of both ethnic types.

Table H1: Average output guesses by participants in complementary study

Participant	Individual workers		Teams		
	Danish-sounding	Muslim-sounding	Danish-sounding	Muslim-sounding	Hetero-geneous
Danish-sounding	109	106	225	220	223
Muslim-sounding	101	98	215	207	211

Notes: The table shows the average guesses for output of individuals and teams by participants in the belief elicitation study with Danish-sounding ($n = 204$) and Muslim-sounding ($n = 149$) names.

Appendix I: Decomposition of the earnings gap

This appendix describes how we decompose the earnings gap in treatment NoInfo into an animus-driven and a belief-driven component in section 4.3B. The earnings gap is the difference in decision makers' total earnings between the benchmark case of accurate statistical discrimination (ASD) and observed earnings. A gap results if decision makers choose a worker of the on average less productive type. Such a choice can result from holding a biased belief about the average price by type, from animus against a type of worker, or from other sources (unexplained part). ASD is profit-maximizing given available information and assumes that any prejudice is absent. That is, ASD assumes decision makers have rational beliefs on the price of discrimination and no animus.

Rational expectations ($Price_i^{RE}$) are determined for each i of the $n = 37$ decision makers as follows. We draw two co-workers (of the same gender as i) from the population of workers in our experiment (161 other workers, see table 1). We estimate team output with each drawn co-worker using i's production in round 1 and model A in table 2. The price of discrimination is then the difference in i's estimated earnings with either type. We repeat this procedure 1'000 times to obtain a distribution of $Price_i^{RE}$.

Elicited expectations ($Price_i^{EE}$) are determined in the same way as in the case of rational expectations except that we do not draw from the true distribution of round 1 output but from the distribution of elicited beliefs about round 1 output. Beliefs are elicited for 353 participants in the belief elicitation study (see section 4.3).

We use the means of these distributions (μ_i^{RE} and μ_i^{EE}, respectively) to predict behavior for i in 4 scenarios which differ by expectations formation (rational vs. elicited) and animus (no vs. as measured in treatment Info). The difference between the benchmark case of ASD and observed outcomes is decomposed into an animus-driven and a belief-driven component (see also section 4.3).

Absent any animus and assuming rational expectations, i chooses *same* if $\mu_i^{RE} < 0$ and *other* otherwise. The case is analogous for elicited expectations and no animus: i chooses *same* if $\mu_i^{EE} < 0$ and *other* otherwise. Note that as long as μ_i^{RE} and μ_i^{EE} have the same sign, they yield the same prediction for the choice of partner. In particular, we find that $\mu_i^{RE} < 0$ and $\mu_i^{EE} < 0$ for all decision makers with Danish-sounding names, and $\mu_i^{RE} > 0$ and $\mu_i^{EE} > 0$ for all decision makers with Muslim-sounding names.

To predict behavior in the case with animus, we feed μ_i^{RE} and μ_i^{EE} into model 1 from table 3 to calculate the probability that i chooses the co-worker of the same ethnic type ($Prob_i^{RE}$ and $Prob_i^{EE}$). We use these probabilities to calculate expected earnings and report earnings foregone by ethnic type from deviating from ASD in each scenario in table 4. Note that because $\mu_i^{RE} \neq \mu_i^{EE}$, and because our estimate of the demand for discrimination is continous (see figure 2), taking biased beliefs into account changes predictions for both ethnic types given animus-based prejudice in table 4.